SPECTOR'S Pins of the World

BEACON HILL PUBLISHING, INC.
ARLINGTON, VIRGINIA
WWW.BEACONHILL-PUBLISHING.COM

Spector's Pins of the World
Edited by Harry Spector and Judy Gold
First Printing, December 1997

Beacon Hill Publishing, Inc
Arlington, VA
(703) 516-4667
WWW.BeaconHill-Publishing.Com

Notice to our Readers

References to "gold," "silver," "bronze," or any other metal are used only to describe color, and not production material.

Phone numbers listed on the backstamps of pins have been deleted from the backstamp descriptions used in this book. If a phone number is stamped on the back of a pin it is represented in this book as <phone#>. "<phone#>" is not part of the actual backstamp. When a backstamp contains text on multiple lines it is shown in this book by a "/." "/" is not part of the actual backstamp unless noted.

Pins are shown approximate actual size, although a few could be as much as 15% percent larger than normal.

Notice of Copyright

Notice of Liability

The information in this book is distributed on an "As Is" basis, without warranty, actual, or implied. Although great care was taken in the preparation of this book, neither the editors, Beacon Hill Publishing, Inc, or any contributor, shall have any liability to any person or entity with respect to any loss or damage caused or alleged to be caused directly or indirectly by the information and/or illustrations contained in this book, or by the resources described in it.

The prices and illustrations in this book are shown for collector's reference only. They do not constitute an offer by the editors, Beacon Hill Publishing, Inc., or any contributor, to buy, sell, or trade any pin illustrated, and should not be construed as such.

ISBN 1-890968-00-5

Printed and bound in the United States of America

Acknowledgments

You would not be reading this guide if it was not for the help of many of our pin collecting friends. We are ever grateful to everyone who gave their time to make this project a reality. We especially want to single out a few people who went above and beyond and then some:

Gary and Mary "M.J." Gettman, who volunteered for the unenviable task of proofing the final copy, loaned us their huge collection, and proved to be an invaluable source of information.

Mario Avila, Lloyd Haas, Craig Perlow, & Steve Robie, who in our opinion, went way out of there way to provide us with their large and valuable collection of hard-to-find pins, and supplied us with more information than we had pages to print it on.

We would also like to thank the following people who loaned us pins, gave us information, or guided us on the current value of the pins included in this guide:

Dan Benson
Bill "Boomer" Blomgren
Tom Brooke (American Pin Collection)
Larry Ehmer
Jim Greensfelder
Bill Hipson
Rick Holman
Issac "Jake" Hunter
Bob Izzy
Josh Jackson (Pindemonium magazine)
Yari Kaveh
Carmen Perrotta
Harald Von Selzam

Photography by CMYK DIgital, Atlanta, Georgia

Editors' Note

You are holding a little piece of history in your hands. While it pales in comparison to Jesse Owens' Gold Medal sprint at Berlin in 1936, or Mark Spitz's record five gold medals in Montreal in 1976 it is, nonetheless, the first professionally produced color national sports committee and "Bid" pin guide (at least to our knowledge). This guide's existence reveals how far, how fast the lapel pin collecting hobby has grown since Don Bigsby and friends founded the pin club, Olympin, some 15 years ago.

To be sure, many pin guides have been produced in the past years, but most of them were dedicated to sponsor and commemorative pins, and only a few of those were produced professionally and distributed outside the inner circle of the hobby. With this guide we illustrate some of the the most collectible and interesting pins in the hobby and all the while exposing the sheer joy of collecting and trading pins to people everywhere.

It might be that you suddenly become enamored with a pin of the ever adorable "Willy," mascot of the Australian Olympic Committee. Or perhaps it causes you to notice the "bid" pin you picked up at the Salt Lake City airport a few years ago for a few bucks is not exactly your average bauble. What ever the reason, we hope you find this book enjoyable and informative, and more importantly allows you to feel more comfortable buying, selling and trading pins.

A great deal of time and effort was put into the production of this book by a lot of people to whom we are forever grateful. We've tried to fit in as many pins, and as much information as the space we had available to us. Unfortunately, this meant a few pins which were discovered after our initial photography session were left out of this edition. Please don't view this as a slight to these pins, but rather as a simple lack of space to place them . We hope to get them in a future edition.

There were also a few pins we knew existed while we were compiling our initial list, but could not locate samples in time to be photographed. We felt is was better to at least acknowledge them in text than to ignore them completely.

We welcome your comments and suggestions to make future editions even better. You can e-mail us at suggestions@BeaconHill-Publishing.com .

Happy Pin Collecting,

Harry Spector & Judy Gold, Editors
Atlanta, Georgia
December 1997

P.S. We have included a brief lapel pin resource list in the back of the book to help you further your interest in the hobby.

How To Use This Guide

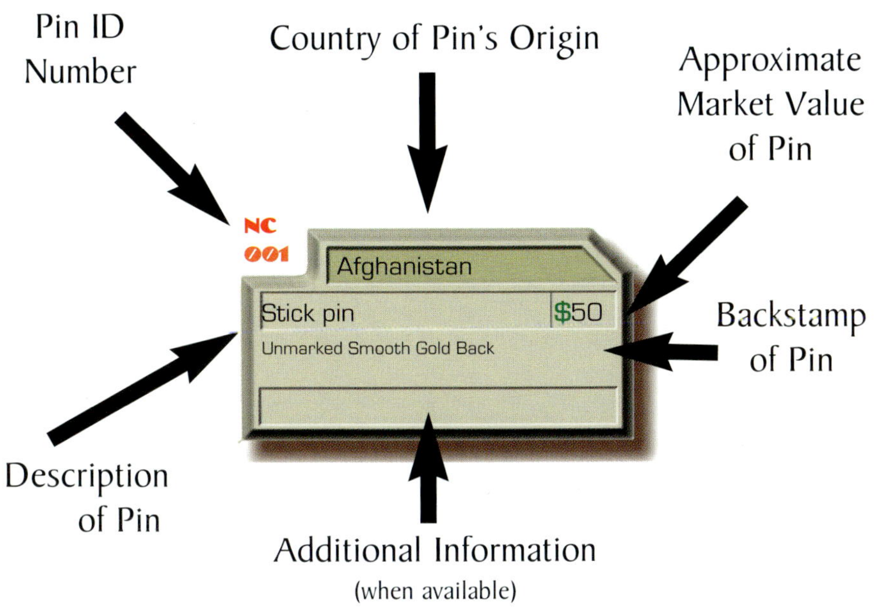

Pin ID Number: This number corresponds to the picture of the pin of the same number on the opposite page. All "National Committee" pins start with "NC," and all "Bid" pins start with "BD."

Country of Pin's Origin: This tells you what country this pin represents. It may or may not have been produced in that country.

Approximate Market Value: This is roughly what the pictured pin is worth as of the printing of this guide. The values printed in this guide are an average of all of the prices suggested by a cross section of dealers and collectors. Prices can vary as much as 20% between dealers.

Backstamp: This is what is printed on the back of the pin or if there is no stamp or marking, how it visually appears.

Additional Information: When available, information about the pin, or a similar pin is printed here.

Notes

National Sports Committees

NC001

NC002

NC003

NC004

NC005

NC006

NC007

NC008

NC009

NC010

NC011

Sorry, Photo of This Pin Is Not Available

NC012

NC 001 — Afghanistan

Stick pin	$50

Unmarked Smooth Gold Back

NC 002 — Albania

Dated D'ble Head Eagle	$55

Unmarked Smooth Gold Back

NC 003 — Albania

Gen'ric D'ble Head Eagle	$35

Unmarked Smooth Gold Back

NC 004 — Algeria

Algerian/US flags /Dove	$8

Algeria/TM,©1992 ACOG/36 USC 380/Pin Society Exclusive/AMINCO/CHINA

NC 005 — Algeria

Grn/Wht Map of Algeria	$21

Tm© 1992 ACOG

NC 006 — American Samoa

Dated Butterfly	$26

© ASNOC 1995

NC 007 — American Samoa

Gold Shield	$18

Unmarked Smooth Gold Back

NC 008 — American Samoa

Shield	$19

36 USC 380/AMINCO/<Phone#>/CHINA

NC 009 — Andorra

Shield / Torchmark	$30

Unmarked Smooth Gold Back

Part of set w/ 6 other pictogram pins (not shown)

NC 010 — Angola

Laurel & Rotor	$20

®/#/36 USC 380/ANGOLA/<Phone #>/CHINA

NC 011 — Antigua-Barbuda

Antiguan Flag/ Sun	$11

ANTIGUA-BARBUDA/TM,©1992 ACOG/36 USC 380/Pin Society Exclusive/AMINCO/CHINA

NC 012 — Antigua-Barbuda

Round Crest	$

NC013

NC014

NC015

NC016

NC017

NC018

NC019

NC020

NC021

NC022

NC023

NC024

NC 013 — Antigua-Barbuda
Small Flag — $13
Unmarked Smooth Gold Back
Dated Atlanta version also made

NC 014 — Argentina
Shield/ Rings & Crest — $16
Unmarked Smooth Gold Back
Domed version also produced

NC 015 — Argentina
Shield / Torchmark — $35
BARRAZA <Phone#> printed in black ink

NC 016 — Argentina
White Rec. / Flag — $9
ARGENTINA/TM,©1992 ACOG/36 USC 380/Pin Society Exclusive/AMINCO/CHINA

NC 017 — Armenia
"Envoy" — $16
Olympic Committee of the/Armenian Republic

NC 018 — Armenia
White Circle — $13
Olympic Committe Of The Armenian Republic
"1996" version also made

NC 019 — Aruba
Blue Oval — $40
Unmarked Smooth Gold Back

NC 020 — Aruba
White Circle — $10
Olympic Committee of the Armenian Republic

NC 021 — Australia
Australian Flag — $21
Unmarked Smooth Gold Back

NC 022 — Australia
Gold 'Roo & Emu — $26
Unmarked Smooth Gold Back

NC 023 — Australia
Map / Aus. Flag — $11
AUSTRALIA/TM,©1992 ACOG/36 USC 380/Pin Society Exclusive/AMINCO/CHINA

NC 024 — Australia
'Roo, Willy, & Aus. Flag — $26
AUST OLYMPIC C'TEE

NC025

NC026

NC027

NC028

NC029

NC030

NC031

NC032

NC033

NC034

NC035

NC036

NC 025 — Australia

Sm. Flag/ Color Rings	$11

Unmarked Smooth Gold Back

NC 026 — Australia

Sm. Flag/ Gold Rings	$8

Unmarked Smooth Gold Back

NC 027 — Australia

Willy / Flag on T-Shirt	$25

CASHS

NC 028 — Austria

Blue Oval / Eagle	$17

Unmarked Smooth Gold Back

NC 029 — Austria

Semi-Star Burst	$15

stobbe/GRAZ-AUSTRIA

NC 030 — Azerbaijan

Small Flag	$67

Unmarked Smooth Gold Back

NC 031 — Bahamas

Dated Shield	$31

No Backstamp. Smooth Gold Back.

NC 032 — Bahamas

Generic Shield $20	

Unmarked Smooth Gold Back

NC 033 — Bahrain

Gold Circle	$22

Unmarked Smooth Gold Back

NC 034 — Bahrain

Gold Rounded Rectangle	$22

Unmarked Smooth Gold Back

NC 035 — Bangladesh

Blue & White Circle	$25

Unmarked Crosshatch Grid

NC 036 — Bangladesh

Flag / Torchmark	$25

Unmarked Smooth Gold Back

Federation Pin

NC037

NC038

Sorry, Photo of This Pin Is Not Available

NC039

NC040

NC041

Sorry, Photo of This Pin Is Not Available

NC042

NC043

NC044

NC045

NC046

NC047

NC048

NC 037 — Barbados

Blue & Yellow Square	$
Unmarked Crosshatch Grid	

NC 038 — Barbados

Rec. Flag / Torchmark	$20
Unmarked Gold Back / Squares	

NC 039 — Belarus

Cyrillic	$

NC 040 — Belarus

Wht. Shld/ Rngs/Flag	$13
Trofe/Lillehammer (on top) • ©1994 BELARUS/Official Licensed Product	

NC 041 — Belarus

Wht. Shld / Torchmark	$10
Trofe/Lillehammer on top • © 1994 BELARUS/Official Licensed Product	

NC 042 — Belgium

Cloisonne Crest	$

NC 043 — Belgium

Crest / Black Bkgrnd	$15
BELGIUM/36 USC 380/Pin Society Exclusive/AMINCO/CHINA	

NC 044 — Belgium

Dated Stripes	$75
No Backstamp. Smooth Gold Back.	

NC 045 — Belgium

Generic Stripes	$10
No Backstamp. Smooth Gold Back.	

NC 046 — Belgium

Sm. Crest -Blue Bkgrnd	$15
Unmarked Smooth Gold Back	

NC 047 — Belgium

Stripes Inside Stripes	$15
Tm.© 1992 ACOG	

NC 048 — Belize

Blue Shield	$50
Unmarked Smooth Gold Back	

NC049

NC050

NC051

NC052

NC053

NC054

NC055

Sorry, Photo of This Pin Is Not Available

NC056

NC057

NC058

NC059

NC060

NC 049 — Benin

Green Circle — $43

©C.O.B. COTONOU/1985/1 OF 50

NC 050 — Benin

White Shield — $10

BENIN/TM,©1992 ACOG/36 USC 380/Pin Society Exclusive/AMINCO/CHINA

NC 051 — Bermuda

Generic Crest — $23

No Backstamp. Smooth Gold Back.

NC 052 — Bermuda

Triangle Torch — $22

Unmarked Crosshatch Grid

NC 053 — Bhutan

Bird — $35

Unmarked Smooth Gold Back

NC 054 — Bhutan

Orange Circle — $20

Unmarked Smooth Gold Back

NC 055 — Bolivia

Gold Rectangle / Bird — $28

No Backstamp. Semi-Smooth Gold back.

NC 056 — Bolivia

Gold Square — $50

NC 057 — Bosnia-Herzegovina

Crossed Flags — $51

NOC 1996/BOSNIE I HERCEGOVINE/REMEMBER SARAJEVO

NC 058 — Bosnia-Herzegovina

Dated Slivertone Circle — $14

BOSNIE I HERCEGOVINE/NOC 1996

NC 059 — Bosnia-Herzegovina

Slivertone Circle — $31

NC 060 — Bosnia-Herzegovina

White Circle / Shield — $20

©BHOC 1996/TAIWAN

Silver and generic versions also made. "Bertoni" backstamp is from Lillehammer

NC061

NC062

NC063

NC064

NC065

NC066

NC067

NC068

NC069

NC070

NC071

NC072

NC 061
Botswana
Dated Green Circle — $28
ETALEX

NC 062
Botswana
Generic Green Circle — $23
ETALEX

NC 063
Botswana
Silver — $30
*** Lekker® stamped over entire back

NC 064
Brazil
Flag / Rings — $15
Unmarked Smooth Gold Back

NC 065
Brazil
Flag / Rings — $10
BRAZIL/36 USC 380/Pin Society Exclusive/AMINCO/CHINA

NC 066
Brazil
Gold Wreath and Flag — $
BRAZIL/36 USC 380/Pin Society Exclusive/AMINCO/CHINA

NC 067
Brazil
Silver Circle / Green Rim — $10
TM,©1992
ACOG/#556363/AMINCO/CHINA

NC 068
British Virgin Islands
Dated White Circle / Seal — $10
BRITISH VIRGIN ISLANDS/TM,©1992
ACOG/36 USC 380/Pin Society
Exclusive/AMINCO/CHINA

NC 069
British Virgin Islands
Gen. Wht. Circ. / Boat — $18
No Backstamp. Smooth Gold back.
"Atlanta" version $35

NC 070
British Virgin Islands
Gen. Wht. Circ. / Shld — $17
No Backstamp. Smooth Gold back.
"Atlanta" version also made

NC 071
British Virgin Islands
Large Seal / Runner — $10
British Virvin Islands/TM,©1992 ACOG/36 USC 380/Pin Society Exclusive/AMINCO/CHINA

NC 072
British Virgin Islands
Small Seal / Runner — $17
Unmarked Smooth Gold Back
"Atlanta" version $30

NC073

NC074

Sorry, Photo of This Pin Is Not Available

NC075

NC076

NC077

Sorry, Photo of This Pin Is Not Available

NC078

NC079

NC080

NC081

NC082

NC083

NC084

NC 073 — Brunel Darussalam
Flag / Rings — $41
Unmarked Smooth Gold Back
Also with filled Rings

NC 074 — Brunel Darussalam
Hands — $57
Unmarked Crosshatch Grid

NC 075 — Bulgaria
Green Circle / Lion — $

NC 076 — Bulgaria
Lion / Cutout Rings — $20
Unmarked Crosshatch Grid

NC 077 — Bulgaria
Lion / Filled Rings — $20
Unmarked Crosshatch Grid

NC 078 — Bulgaria
Red Circle / Lion — $45

NC 079 — Bulgaria
White Circle / Lion — $30

NC 080 — Bulgaria
Wht. Shld - Grn Lion — $12
BULGARIA/TM,©1992 ACOG/36 USC 380/Pin Society Exclusive/AMINCO/CHIN

NC 081 — Bulgaria
Wht Shld-Silver Lion — $15
Unmarked Smooth Gold Back
Made for Atlanta

NC 082 — Burkina Faso
Dated Circle — $9
BURKINA FASO/TM,©1992 ACOG/36 USC 380/Pin Society Exclusive/AMINCO/CHIN

NC 083 — Burkina Faso
Decatur Host — $28
DECATUR/BURKINA, 1996/BY SANCHEZ ENT/TAIWAN
Part of puzzle set w/ NC085

NC 084 — Burkina Faso
Rotor — $50
Unmarked Crosshatch Grid

NC085

NC086

NC087

NC088

NC089

NC090

NC091

NC092

NC093

NC094

NC095

NC096

NC 085 — Burkina Faso

Upside Down Obelisk	$26
C.N.O.S.B 1993/BY SANCHEZ ENT/TAIWAN	
Part of puzzle set w/ NC083	

NC 086 — Burundi

Dated Shield	$10
BURUNDI/TM,©1992 ACOG/36 USC 380/Pin SocietyExclusive/AMINCO/CHINA	

NC 087 — Cambodia

Bronzetone Temple	$19
National Olympic Committee/of Cambodia 1996	

NC 088 — Cambodia

Gold Temple	$40
Unmarked Smooth Gold Back	

NC 089 — Cambodia

Silver Temple	$33
©1996 N.O.C.C./MATTE CANADA	
Also produced in gold ($60)	

NC 090 — Cambodia

Square / Temple	$43
No Backstamp. Smooth Gold Back.	

NC 091 — Cameroon

Rectangle	$34

NC 092 — Canada

"1896-1996"	$14
M inside circle + "COA/AOC"/ARTISS/REGINA/CANADA	

NC 093 — Canada

Atlanta Skyline	$15
M inside circle + "COA/AOC"/ARTISS/REGINA/CANADA	

NC 094 — Canada

Dated Rec.-Maple Lf	$14
M in circle/C.O.A.\A.O.C./ARTISS/REGINA/CANADA	

NC 095 — Canada

Dated Shield	$45
Unmarked Crosshatch Grid	
"Prime Minister's Pin"	

NC 096 — Canada

Gold Maple Leaf Cutout	$12
M in circle/COA/TAIWAN	

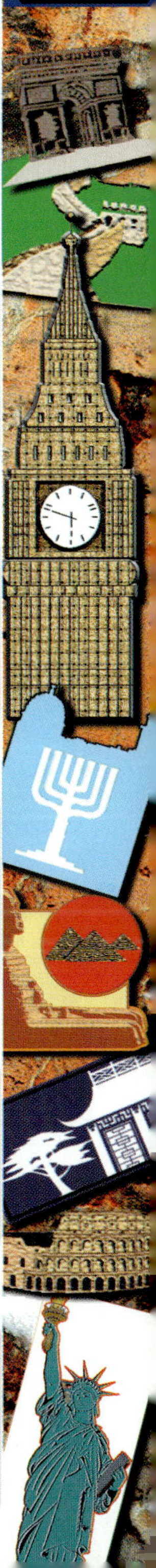

NC097

NC098

NC099

NC100

NC101

NC102

NC103

NC104

NC105

NC106

Sorry, Photo of This Pin Is Not Available

NC107

NC 097 Canada

Maple Leaf	$11
© C.O.A./A.O.C. /ARTISS-REGINA/CHINA	

NC 098 Canada

Maple Leaf Cutout	$9
M in circle/C.O.A.\A.O.C./ARTISS/ REGINA CALGARY/TAIWAN	
Very large version also exists	

NC 099 Canada

Maple Lf Cutout on Rec	$11
M in circle/C.O.A.\A.O.C./ARTISS/ REGINA CALGARY/TAIWAN	

NC 100 Canada

"Merci/Thanks"	$50
M inside circle + "COA/AOC"/ARTISS/REGINA/CANADA	

NC 101 Canada

Moose Mascot	$34
M inside circle + COA/ LAURIE ARTISS LTD./REGINA CALGARY/CANADA	

NC 102 Canada

Pewter Circle/Pictograms	$12
M inside circle + COA/AOC	

NC 103 Cape Verde

Oval / White Ribbon	$8
CAPE VERDE/TM,©1992 ACOG/36 USC 380/Pin Society Exclusive/AMINCO/CHINA	

NC 104 Cape Verde

White Ribbon	$150
No Backstamp. Semi-Smooth Gold Back.	

NC 105 Cayman Islands

Generic Shield	$18
No Backstamp. Raised Squares on Back.	

NC 106 Cayman Islands

Gold Turtle	$55
No Backstamp. Semi-Smooth Gold back.	

NC 107 Central African Republic

	$

NC108

Sorry, Photo of This Pin Is Not Available

NC109

NC110

NC111

NC112

NC113

NC114

NC115

NC116

NC117

NC118

NC119

NC 108 — Central African Republic
White Circle/Wreath — $11
CENTRAL AFRICANREP/TM,©1992 ACOG/36 USC 380/Pin Society Exclusive/AMINCO/CHINA

NC 109 — Chad
Gold Circle / Map — $109
J.BALME/SAUMUR

NC 110 — Chad
Shield — $11
TCHAD/TM,©1992 ACOG/36 USC 380/Pin Society Exclusive/AMINCO/CHINA

NC 111 — Chile
Dated Shield / Cutout Rings — $50
Unmarked Smooth Gold Back

NC 112 — Chile
Dated White Shield — $9
CHILE/TM,©1992 ACOG/36 USC 380/Pin Society Exclusive/AMINCO/CHINA

NC 113 — Chile
Gen. Shld / Blk Rings — $15
MILLED/CHILE

NC 114 — Chile
Gen. Shld / Color Rings — $19
Illegible Mark at Tip

NC 115 — China
Flag / Cutout Rings — $11
Unmarked Smooth Gold Back
Produced for Atlanta

NC 116 — China
Flag / Filled Rings — $17
Unmarked Crosshatch Grid

NC 117 — China
Gold Torchmark — $21
Unmarked Crosshatch Grid

NC 118 — Chinese Taipei
Dated Scollop — $9
CHINESE TAIPEI/TM,©1992 ACOG/36 USC 380/Pin SocietyExclusive/AMINCO/CHINA

NC 119 — Chinese Taipei
Horiz Rec / Torchmark — $11
YOLEEN/FAX<number> stamped in staggered rows

NC120

NC121

NC122

Sorry, Photo of This Pin Is Not Available

NC123

NC124

NC125

NC126

NC127

NC128

NC129

NC130

NC131

NC 120 Chinese Taipei
Scalloped / Rings — $9
No Backstamp. Smooth Gold Back.

NC 121 Columbia
Flag / Torchmark — $27
Unmarked Smooth Gold Back

NC 122 Columbia
Shld / Gldtone Rings — $16
No Backstamp. Smooth Gold Back.

NC 123 Columbia
White Circle / Flag — $

NC 124 Comoros
Generic Green Oval — $
36 USC 380/AMINCO/<Phone#>/CHINA

NC 125 Comoros
Green Circle — $30
UNION MADE/USA inside oval on right edge

NC 126 Comoros
Green Circle/Cutout — $29
36 USC 380/AMINCO/<Phone #>/CHINA

NC 127 Congo
Map / "Congo" — $100

NC 128 Cook Islands
Gold Circle — $33
No Backstamp. Smooth Gold Back.

NC 129 Cook Islands
Gold/Green Circle — $35
Unmarked Smooth Gold Back

NC 130 Cook Islands
Vertical Trapezoid — $8
COOK ISLANDS/TM,©1992 ACOG/36 USC 380/Pin SocietyExclusive/AMINCO/CHINA

NC 131 Costa Rica
Lrg Grn Circle / Shld — $7
COSTA RICA/36 USC 380/Pin Society Exclusive/AMINCO/CHINA

NC132

NC133

NC134

NC135

NC136

NC137

NC138

NC139

NC140

NC141

Sorry, Photo of This Pin Is Not Available

NC142

NC143

NC 132 — Costa Rica
Shield / RIngs — $25
CHUNKOK/KOREA

NC 133 — Costa Rica
Sm Grn Circle / Shld — $16
CHUNKOK/KOREA

NC 134 — Croatia
Flag / Shield — $11
Unmarked Smooth Gold Back

NC 135 — Croatia
Oly Com. Shld-Lg. Rings — $13
Unmarked Crosshatch Grid

NC 136 — Croatia
Oly Com. Shld-Sm. Rings — $13
No Backstamp. Smooth Gold Back.

NC 137 — Croatia
Olympic Team Shield — $13
Unmarked Crosshatch Grid

NC 138 — Croatia
"Pin Society" White Shld — $9

NC 139 — Croatia
Silver Shield — $10
P.P.U./ZAGREB stamped around base of pin

NC 140 — Cuba
Dated Shield / Wreath — $18
Unmarked Smooth Gold Back

NC 141 — Cuba
Flag -Light Blue Stripes — $20
Unmarked Crosshatch Grid

NC 142 — Cuba
Flag / Filled Rings — $15

NC 143 — Cuba
Flg / Drk Bl. Stripes — $15
Unmarked Crosshatch Grid

NC144

NC145

NC146

NC147

NC148

NC149

NC150

NC151

NC152

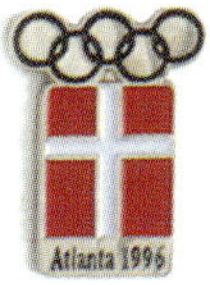

NC153

NC154

NC 144
Cuba
Large Shield $16
No Backstamp. Smooth Gold Back.

NC 145
Cuba
Small Shield $13
Unmarked Smooth Textured Back

NC 146
Cyprus
Dated White Shield $10
CYPRUS/TM,©1992 ACOG/36 USC 380/Pin SocietyExclusive/AMINCO/CHINA

NC 147
Cyprus
Generic White Shield $15
ARECO-CANADA/KOE

NC 148
Czech Republic
Dated Crest / Ribbon $80
Unmarked Smooth Bronzetone Back
Delegation Pin

NC 149
Czech Republic
Dated Crest / Flag $65
Unmarked Smooth Gold Back

NC 150
Czech Republic
Dated Flag $23
No Backstamp. Smooth Gold Back.

NC 151
Czech Republic
Dated Square / Lion $29
ZNAK PHAHA COV 1994
Athlete Participant Pin

NC 152
Czech Republic
Undated Flag $15
Unmarked Smooth Gold Back

NC 153
Denmark
Dated Flag $27
Unmarked Smooth Silver Back

NC 154
Denmark
Generic Flag $12
Unmarked Smooth Gold Back

NC155

NC156

NC157

NC158

NC159

NC160

NC161

NC162

NC163

NC164

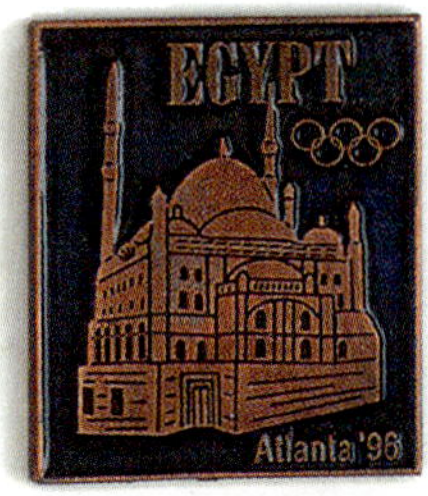

NC165

NC166

NC 155 — Djibouti
Elk Head — $25
MADE IN USA

NC 156 — Djibouti
Elk Head & Cutout Rings — $8
DJIBOUTI/TM,©1992 ACOG/36 USC 380/Pin SocietyExclusive/AMINCO/CHINA

NC 157 — Dominica
Facing Birds — $45
© 1996 D.O.C./MATTE CANADA

NC 158 — Dominican Republic
Palm Tree — $10
MADE IN CANADA

NC 159 — Dominican Republic
Parrot — $10
MADE IN CANADA

NC 160 — Dominican Republic
Three Interlocking Rings Above Five — $13
SIMBA CA INC/MADE IN USA inside small oval on bottom of back

NC 161 — Dominican Republic
White Circle — $9
DOMINCAN REPUBLIC/TM,©1992 ACOG/36 USC 380/Pin Society Exclusive/AMINCO/CHINA

NC 162 — Ecuador
Black Circle/Stylized Eagle — $25
C.O.E.©1994

NC 163 — Ecuador
Dated Yellow Stylized Eagle — $40
C.O.E.©1996

NC 164 — Ecuador
Shield with Eagle — $19
Unmarked Smooth Gold Back

NC 165 — Egypt
Mosque — $6
No Backstamp. Smooth Bronzetone Back.

NC 166 — Egypt
Mythical Winged Person — $6
EGYPT NOC/LIMITED EDITION/OF 1000

NC167

NC168

NC169

NC170

NC171

NC172

NC173

NC174

NC175

NC176

NC177

NC178

NC 167 — Egypt
Pharaoh — $6
EGYPT NOC/LIMITED EDITION/OF 1000

NC 168 — Egypt
Pyramid — $7
MADE IN CANADA

NC 169 — Egypt
Statues — $6
MADE IN CANADA

NC 170 — Egypt
Torchmark — $20
No Backstamp. Smooth Gold Back.

NC 171 — El Salvador
Generic Shield / Rings — $18
No Backstamp. Semi-Smooth Gold Back.

NC 172 — El Salvador
Shield & Torchmark — $9
EL SALVADOR/TM,©1992 ACOG/36 USC 380/Pin SocietyExclusive/AMINCO/CHINA

NC 173 — Equatorial Guinea
Rings / Flame on Top — $10
ECUATORIAL GUINEA/TM,©1992ACOG/36 USC 380/Pin Society Exclusive/AMINCO/CHINA

NC 174 — Estonia
Flag — $15
Unmarked Crosshatch Grid

NC 175 — Estonia
Shld / Gldtone Wreath — $10
ESTONIA/TM,©1992 ACOG/36 USC 380/Pin SocietyExclusive/AMINCO/CHINA

NC 176 — Ethiopia
Dated Rec / Flag — $8
MADE IN CANADA

NC 177 — Ethiopia
Dated Rec/ "WALIA IBEX" — $8
MADE IN CANADA

NC 178 — Ethiopia
Green & Red Circle — $25
S. JOHNSON/ITALY

NC179

Sorry, Photo of This Pin Is Not Available

NC180

NC181

NC182

NC183

NC184

NC185

NC186

NC187

NC188

NC189

NC190

NC 179
Ethiopia
Large Dated Rectangle $10
MADE IN CANADA

NC 180
Ethiopia
Pewter Shield $

NC 181
Ethiopia
"Pin Society" Flag $5

NC 182
Ethiopia
Small Circle $45
Unmarked Smooth Gold Back

NC 183
Ethiopia
Small Dated Rectangle $25
No Backstamp. Rough Gold Back.

NC 184
Fiji
Dated BlueCircle $30
Unmarked Smooth Gold Back

NC 185
Fiji
Generic BlueCircle $10
Unmarked Crosshatch Grid

NC 186
Fiji
Rectangle / Torchmark $
Unmarked Smooth Gold Back

NC 187
Finland
Generic Flag $25
Unmarked Smooth Gold Back

NC 188
France
Dated Cutout Rooster $125
FRAISSE Paris

NC 189
France
Dated Rooster $20
PC PRO/PARIS printed in black ink

NC 190
France
Generic Rooster $15
PC PRO/PARIS printed in black ink

NC191

NC192

NC193

NC194

NC195

NC196

NC197

NC198

NC199

NC200

NC201

NC202

NC 191
Gabon
"Albert Schweitzer" $25
36 USC 380/AMINCO/CHINA

NC 192
Gabon
House of Africa Dangle $9
IMPRINTED PRODUCTS/<Phone#>/SAN DEIGO, CA/MADE IN CHINA

NC 193
Gabon
Large Shield $60
FRAISSR/PARIS

NC 194
Gabon
Small Shield $25
Unmarked Smooth Gold Back

NC 195
Gambia
Scorpions $10
THE GAMBIA/36 USC 380/Pin Society Exclusive/AMINCO/CHINA

NC 196
Georgia
Blue Rectangle $8

NC 197
Georgia
Blue Rectangle-Torchmk $10

NC 198
Georgia
Bronze Swordsman $8
GEORGIA NOC/LIMITED EDITION/OF 200

NC 199
Georgia
Crossed Flgs-"GNOC ..." $15
36 USC 380/AMINCO/CHINA

NC 200
Georgia
Day 01 $7
GEORGIA NOC/LIMITED TO/500 SETS

NC 201
Georgia
Day 02 $7
GEORGIA NOC/LIMITED TO/500 SETS

NC 202
Georgia
Day 03 $7
GEORGIA NOC/LIMITED TO/500 SETS

NC203

NC204

NC205

NC206

NC207

NC208

NC209

NC210

NC211

NC212

NC213

NC214

NC 203 — Georgia
Day 04 — $7
GEORGIA NOC/LIMITED TO/500 SETS

NC 204 — Georgia
Day 05 — $7
GEORGIA NOC/LIMITED TO/500 SETS

NC 205 — Georgia
Day 06 — $7
GEORGIA NOC/LIMITED TO/500 SETS

NC 206 — Georgia
Day 07 — $7
GEORGIA NOC/LIMITED TO/500 SETS

NC 207 — Georgia
Day 08 — $7
GEORGIA NOC/LIMITED TO/500 SETS

NC 208 — Georgia
Day 09 — $7
GEORGIA NOC/LIMITED TO/500 SETS

NC 209 — Georgia
Day 10 — $7
GEORGIA NOC/LIMITED TO/500 SETS

NC 210 — Georgia
Day 11 — $7
GEORGIA NOC/LIMITED TO/500 SETS

NC 211 — Georgia
Day 12 — $7
GEORGIA NOC/LIMITED TO/500 SETS

NC 212 — Georgia
Day 13 — $7
GEORGIA NOC/LIMITED TO/500 SETS

NC 213 — Georgia
Day 14 — $7
GEORGIA NOC/LIMITED TO/500 SETS

NC 214 — Georgia
Day 15 — $7
GEORGIA NOC/LIMITED TO/500 SETS

NC215

NC216

NC217

NC218

NC219

NC220

NC221

NC222

NC223

NC224

NC225

NC226

NC 215 — Georgia

Day 16 — $7

GEORGIA NOC/LIMITED TO/500 SETS

NC 216 — Georgia

Day 17 — $7

GEORGIA NOC/LIMITED TO/500 SETS

NC 217 — Georgia

GOC Logo and Peach — $8

Unmarked Crosshatch Grid

NC 218 — Georgia

Red/Blue & Swordsman — $9

GEORGIA NOC/LIMITED EDITION/OF 2000

NC 219 — Georgia

Shld / Dragon & Knight — $11

Unmarked Crosshatch Grid

NC 220 — Georgia

"Two Georgias" (Large) — $21

GEORGIA NOC/LIMITED EDITION/ OF 500

NC 221 — Georgia

"Two Georgias" (Small) — $11

Unmarked Crosshatch Grid

NC 222 — Georgia

White Rectangle — $9

Trofe/Lillehammer stamped above pin. © 1994 G.O.C./Officially licensed product.

NC 223 — Georgia

White Rectangle/Trchmk — $12

Trofe/Lillehammer stamped above pin. © 1994 G.O.C./Officially licensed product.

NC 224 — Germany

Dated Eagle — $13

SORGEL/27612 LOXSTEDT/TEL<Phone #>

NC 225 — Germany

Generic Eagle — $16

METZEN/MUNCHEN

Stick pin

NC 226 — Germany

Map / Torchmark — $13

GERMANY/TM,©1992 ACOG/36 USC 380/Pin SocietyExclusive/AMINCO/CHINA

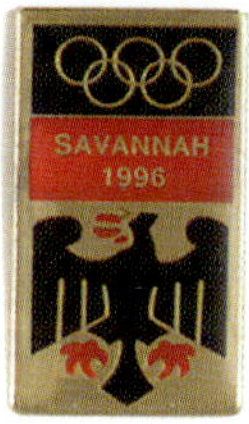

NC227

NC228

NC229

NC230

NC231

NC232

NC233

NC234

NC235

NC236

NC237

NC238

NC 227 — Germany
Savannah — $41

NC 228 — Ghana
Large Blue Background — $18
©G.O.C./ATLANTA 1996

NC 229 — Ghana
Large Red, Yellow & Grn — $20
©G.O.C./ATLANTA 1996

NC 230 — Ghana
Light Blue Background — $18
FC'96

NC 231 — Ghana
Red, Orange,& Grn Shld — $12
GHANA/TM,©1992 ACOG/36 USC 380/Pin SocietyExclusive/AMINCO/CHINA

NC 232 — Ghana
Small Blue Background — $18
©G.O.C./ATLANTA 1996

NC 233 — Ghana
Small Red, Yellow & Grn — $18
©G.O.C./ATLANTA 1996

NC 234 — Great Britain
"100 YEARS..." — $10
GREAT BRITAIN/TM,©1992 ACOG/36 USC 380/Pin SocietyExclusive/AMINCO/CHINA

NC 235 — Great Britain
1896 Shield — $10
GREAT BRITAIN/TM,©1992 ACOG/36 USC 380/Pin Society Exclusive/MADE FOR '96 OLYMPICS/ AMINCO/CHINA

NC 236 — Great Britain
1908 Repro. Badge — $10
GREAT BRITAN/TM,©1992 ACOG/36 USC 380/Pin Society Exclusive/MADE FOR '96 OLYMPICS/ AMINCO/CHINA

NC 237 — Great Britain
1948 Repro. Badge — $10
GREAT BRITAN/TM,©1992 ACOG/36 USC 380/Pin Society Exclusive/MADE FOR '96 OLYMPICS/ AMINCO/CHINA

NC 238 — Great Britain
Blk Oval / Lion — $14
Unmarked Smooth Gold Back

NC239

NC240

NC241

NC242

NC243

NC244

NC245

NC246

NC247

NC248

NC249

NC250

NC 239 — Great Britain
Blk Rec/ "1996 Atlanta" — $14
Unmarked Smooth Gold Back

NC 240 — Great Britain
Blk Rec./Discus Thrower — $14
Unmarked Smooth Gold Back

NC 241 — Great Britain
Blk Rec / Man — $14
Unmarked Smooth Gold Back

NC 242 — Great Britain
Blk Rectangle / Torch — $14
Unmarked Smooth Gold Back

NC 243 — Great Britain
Cut-out Stylized Lion — $11
GREAT BRITAIN/36 USC 380/Pin Society Exclusive/AMINCO/CHINA

NC 244 — Great Britain
Dated Shield — $20
No Backstamp. Semi-Smooth Silver Back.

NC 245 — Great Britain
Dated Square Lion — $21
Unmarked Crosshatch Grid

NC 246 — Great Britain
Flag w Torchmrk & GB — $16
GREAT BRITAIN/TM,©1992 ACOG/36 USC 380/Pin SocietyExclusive/AMINCO/CHINA

NC 247 — Great Britain
Oval Lion- GoldRings — $18

NC 248 — Great Britain
Oval Lion-Color Rings — $13
No Backstamp. Smooth Gold Back.

NC 249 — Great Britain
"Team Britain" — $13
Unmarked Smooth Gold Back

NC 250 — Greece
Shield — $11
No Backstamp. Smooth Gold back.

NC251

NC252

Sorry, Photo of This Pin Is Not Available

NC253

NC254

NC255

NC256

NC257

NC258

NC259

NC260

NC261

NC262

NC 251 — Greece

Silver Rec / Runner	$25
Unmarked Smooth Silver Back	

NC 252 — Grenada

Dated Flag	$18
Unmarked Smooth Gold Back	

NC 253 — Grenada

Generic Flag	$15

NC 254 — Grenada

Hour Glass Shape & Flg	$5
GRENADA/TM,©1992 ACOG/36 USC 380/Pin SocietyExclusive/AMINCO/CHINA	

NC 255 — Guam

Oval / Palm Tree	$15
GIFT CREATIONS/MADE IN TAIWAN	

NC 256 — Guam

"Team Guam"	$15
36 USC 380/CHINA	

NC 257 — Guam

Two Torchrunners	$60
36 USC 380/MADE IN CHINA	

NC 258 — Guam

"USA Olympics..."	$60
36 USC 380/MADE IN CHINA	

NC 259 — Guatemala

Blue Deleg. / Trchmk	$35
No Backstamp. Smooth Gold Back.	

NC 260 — Guatemala

Lt Blue Circle	$10
No Backstamp. Smooth Gold back.	

NC 261 — Guatemala

Purple Deleg / Trchmk	$25
Unmarked Smooth Gold Back	

NC 262 — Guinea

Crossing Sword & Rifle	$5
GUINEA/TM,©1992 ACOG/36 USC 380/Pin SocietyExclusive/AMINCO/CHINA	

Sorry, Photo of This Pin Is Not Available

NC263

NC264

NC265

NC266

NC267

NC268

Sorry, Photo of This Pin Is Not Available

NC269

NC270

NC271

NC272

NC273

NC274

NC 263
Guinea
Elephant $50

NC 264
Guinea Bissau
Colored Torch $21
36 USC 380/AMINCO/<Phone#>/CHINA

NC 265
Guinea Bissau
Gold Torch $31
© 1996 COGBS/ED. SPECIALE 150/MATTE CANADA

NC 266
Guyana
Dated Rectangle $20
No Backstamp. Semi-Smooth Gold Back.

NC 267
Honduras
Wht. Circ on Top of Flg $16
LEPINGLEBIE/CANOIAC, QUEBEC

NC 268
Hong Kong
Blue Crest $16
G.C.I./MADE IN TAIWAN

NC 269
Hungary
Crest on Silver Shield/Rings $21
No Backstamp. Smooth Silver Back.

NC 270
Hungary
Crest / Ribbon $58
434

NC 271
Hungary
Rings on Flag $
Unmarked Smooth Gold Back

NC 272
Iceland
Geyser $20
Unmarked Smooth Gold Back

NC 273
India
Flag / Gold Rings $10
Unmarked Smooth Gold Back

NC 274
India
Flag / Silver Rings $10
Unmarked Smooth Silver Back

NC275

Sorry, Photo of This Pin Is Not Available

NC276

NC277

NC278

NC279

NC280

NC281

NC282

NC283

NC284

Sorry, Photo of This Pin Is Not Available

NC285

NC286

NC 275 — India
"India" / Rings — $10
TEJ BROS ©

NC 276 — India
Round "Ind. Oly. Assoc" — $11

NC 277 — India
White Oval — $11
INDIA/36 USC 380/Pin Society Exclusive/AMINCO/CHINA

NC 278 — Indonesia
Red/Wht. Circ / Eagle — $17
Unmarked Smooth Gold Back

NC 279 — Indonesia
Triangle / Eagle — $29
Unmarked Smooth Gold Back

NC 280 — Iran
Green, Wht, Red Flame — $28
No Backstamp. Semi-Smooth Gold Back.

NC 281 — Iraq
Inverted "J" — $27
Unmarked Smooth Gold Back

NC 282 — Iraq
Pewter Lion/Man — $45
Unmarked Smooth Silver Back

NC 283 — Ireland
Shamrock / Rings — $8
Unmarked Crosshatch Grid

NC 284 — Ireland
St. Patty's Day '95 — $5

NC 285 — Ireland
St. Patty's Day '96 — $13

NC 286 — Ireland
Wht Circ / Shamrock — $15
IRELAND/TM,©1992 ACOG/36 USC 380/Pin SocietyExclusive/AMINCO/CHINA

NC287

NC288

NC289

NC290

NC291

Sorry, Photo of This Pin Is Not Available

NC292

NC293

Sorry, Photo of This Pin Is Not Available

NC294

Sorry, Photo of This Pin Is Not Available

NC295

NC296

NC297

NC298

NC 287 — Ireland

Wht Shld / Shamrock — $12

Unmarked Crosshatch Grid

NC 288 — Israel

4-Pin Puzzle Set — $35

©I.O.C. + set number

Torchmark use not auth. by ACOG

NC 289 — Israel

Blue Rec / Torchmk — $9

NC 290 — Israel

Drk Bl Shld / Menorah — $10

Unmarked Smooth Gold Back

NC 291 — Israel

Dated Shld / Menorah — $10

ISRAEL/TM,©1992 ACOG/36 USC 380/Pin SocietyExclusive/AMINCO/CHINA

NC 292 — Israel

Grey Rec / Trchmk — $10

NC 293 — Israel

Lt Blu Shld/ Menorah — $10

Unmarked Smooth Silver Back

NC 294 — Israel

Peach / Torchmark — $10

NC 295 — Israel

Red Rec / Torchmark — $10

NC 296 — Israel

Stylized Flg / Rings — $10

NC 297 — Israel

White Circle / Menorah — $10

Unmarked Smooth Gold Back

NC 298 — Israel

White Sq. / Menorah — $10

Unmarked Smooth Gold Back

NC299

NC300

NC301

NC302

NC303

NC304

NC305

NC306

NC307

NC308

NC309

NC310

NC 299 Israel
White Sq. / Menorah — $10
Unmarked Smooth Gold Back

NC 300 Italy
Cutout Rngs/Blue Str on top — $15
BERTONI-MILANO

NC 301 Italy
Small Cutout Rings — $14
BERTONI-MILANO

NC 302 Italy
Torchmark / Flags — $16
No Backstamp. Semi-Smooth Gold Back.

NC 303 Ivory Coast
Shield / Elephant — $45
Unmarked Smooth Gold Back
Not used for Atlanta

NC 304 Jamaica
Flag on Shield — $12
Unmarked Smooth Gold Back

NC 305 Jamaica
White Shield / Flag — $12
JAMAICA/TM,©1992 ACOG/36 USC 380/Pin SocietyExclusive/AMINCO/CHINA

NC 306 Japan
Sm Flg-Gold Rings — $23
Unmarked Smooth Gold Back

NC 307 Japan
Sm Flg-Silvertne Rings — $10
No Backstamp. Smooth Silver Back.

NC 308 Japan
Thumbnail Size Flag — $10
No Backstamp. Smooth Silver Back.

NC 309 Jordan
Green, White, & Black "J" — $24
Unmarked Smooth Gold Back

NC 310 Kazakhstan
Light Blue Flag / Rings — $10
36 USC 380/REPUBLIC OF KAZA-KHSTAN/1996 Olympic Games Pin Society

NC311

NC312

NC313

NC314

NC315

NC316

Sorry, Photo of This Pin Is Not Available

NC317

Sorry, Photo of This Pin Is Not Available

NC318

NC319

Sorry, Photo of This Pin Is Not Available

NC320

NC321

NC322

NC 311 Kazakhstan
Med. Blue Flag / RIngs | $
Tm.©1992 ACOG

NC 312 Kenya
Lions / Banner | $17
No Backstamp. Rough Gold Back.

NC 313 Kenya
Lions / Map | $40

NC 314 Kuwait
Camel | $45
No Backstamp. Smooth Silver Back.

NC 315 Kuwait
Horse | $45
Unmarked Smooth Gold Back

NC 316 Kuwait
Eagle / Shield | $25
Unmarked Smooth Gold Back

NC 317
This Pin Was Removed

NC 318 Kuwait
Ship | $35

NC 319 Kyrgyzstan
Horse In Mountains | $10
KYRGYZSTAN/TM,©1992 ACOG/36 USC 380/Pin SocietyExclusive/AMINCO/CHINA

NC 320 Kyrgyzstan
Mountains / Pictograms | $
No Rings

NC 321 Kyrgyzstan
Mountains/Running Horse | $72
Unmarked Smooth Gold Back

NC 322 Laos
Dated Flag | $8
LAOS/TM,©1992 ACOG/36 USC 380/Pin Society Exclusive/AMINCO/CHINA

NC323

NC324

NC325

NC326

NC327

NC328

NC329

NC330

NC331

NC 323
Laos
Flag — $25
Unmarked Smooth Gold Back

NC 324
Latvia
Dated Ribbon — $25

NC 325
Latvia
Dated Ribbon Pin/Pin — $25
LATIVA/TM,©1992 ACOG/36 USC 380/PIN SOCIETY EXCLUSIVE/AMINCO/CHINA

NC 326
Latvia
Generic Pin on Pin Ribbon — $20
ATVTAL/36 USC 380/AMINCO/<Phone #>/CHINA

NC 327
Latvia
Ribbon — $10
LATVIA/36 USC 380/Pin Society Exclusive/AMINCO/CHINA

NC 328
Lebanon
Shield / Cyprus Tree — $40
Unmarked Smooth Gold Back

NC 329
Lesotho
Horse / Rider — $75

NC 330
Liberia
White Circle — $9
LIBERIA/TM,©1992 ACOG/36 USC 380/Pin SocietyExclusive/AMINCO/CHINA

NC 331
Libya
Dark Green Circle — $92
Flowers

NC332

NC333

NC334

NC335

NC336

NC337

NC338

NC339

NC340

NC341

NC342

NC 332 Liechtenstein

Crown / Rings — $11

MADE BY FITTECH/INUCIRIES/FOR GUADRI B.V./TEL <number>

NC 333 Lithuania

Dated "Lietuva" Shield — $19

No Backstamp. Smooth Gold Back.

NC 334 Lithuania

"Lietuva" / Torchmark — $10

LITHUANIA/TM,©1992 ACOG/36 USC 380/Pin SocietyExclusive/AMINCO/CHINA

NC 335 Lithuania

White Cirlce / "Lietuva" — $15

Unmarked Smooth Gold Back

NC 336 Luxembourg

Dated Lion & Crown — $28

Pretty Things

NC 337 Luxembourg

Shield/Cutout Crwn/ Rings — $18

No Backstamp. Rough Gold Crosshatch back.

NC 338 Luxembourg

Shield / Cutout Crwn & Rings — $20

©G.C.I./M.I.T.

Stickpin

NC 339 Luxembourg

Thumbnail Size Shield — $23

DETROIT PRODUCTION/00352-595072

NC 340 Macedonia

Red Mountains (Small) — $50

Unmarked Smooth Gold Back

Large Version $75

NC 341 Madacascar

Shield — $300

Unmarked Smooth Silver Back

NC 342 Malawi

Circle w/Flag — $50

NC343

NC344

NC345

NC346

NC347

Sorry, Photo of This Pin Is Not Available

NC348

NC349

NC350

Sorry, Photo of This Pin Is Not Available

NC351

NC352

NC353

NC354

NC 343 — Malawi

Flag Inside Wreath — $12

MALAWI/TM,©1992 ACOG/36 USC 380/Pin SocietyExclusive/AMINCO/CHINA

NC 344 — Malaysia

Circle / Flag & Rings — $16

No Backstamp. Smooth Silver Back.

NC 345 — Malaysia

Circle / Flag & Trchmk — $15

No Backstamp. Smooth Gold Back.

NC 346 — Malaysia

Cutout IZZY Flag — $18

No Backstamp. Smooth Gold Back.

NC 347 — Malaysia

Dated Rectangle — $10

MALAYSIA/TM,©1992 ACOG/36 USC 380/Pin SocietyExclusive/AMINCO/CHINA

NC 348 — Malaysia

Generic Rectangle — $15

Unmarked Smooth Gold Back

NC 349 — Malaysia

Round IZZY Flag — $15

No Backstamp. Smooth Gold Back.

NC 350 — Malaysia

Waving Flag / Rings — $14

No Backstamp. Smooth Gold back.

NC 351 — Maldives

Blue Committee — $18

NC 352 — Maldives

Dated Flag — $23

No Backstamp. Semi-Smooth Silver Back / Crosshatch pattern.

NC 353 — Maldives

Wht Circ / Flg & Rings — $20

No Backstamp. Smooth Gold back.

NC 354 — Mali

Shield — $20

©G.C.I./MADE IN TAIWAN

NC355

NC356

NC357

NC358

Sorry, Photo of This Pin Is Not Available

NC359

Sorry, Photo of This Pin Is Not Available

NC360

NC361

NC362

NC363

NC364

NC365

NC366

NC 355
Malta
Dated Red Cross $8
MALTA/TM,©1992 ACOG/36 USC 380/Pin SocietyExclusive/AMINCO/CHINA

NC 356
Malta
Red Cross $13
Unmarked Crosshatch Grid

NC 357
Mauritania
Shield $8
Mauritania/ TM,©1992 ACOG/36 USC 380/Pin SocietyExclusive/AMINCO/CHINA

NC 358
Mauritius
White Circle on Red Triangle $8
Mauritius/TM,©1992 ACOG/36 USC 380/Pin SocietyExclusive/AMINCO/CHINA

NC 359
Mexico
Black Circle $12

NC 360
Mexico
Blue Circle $12

NC 361
Mexico
Dated White Rec/Gld Circle $
Tm,© 1992 ACOG

NC 362
Mexico
Generic White Rec/ Gld Circ $
Unmarked Smooth Gold Back

NC 363
Mexico
Gold Circle /Torch & Flag $23
CABRE F MEX®. Various pictgrams are also stamped on back

NC 364
Mexico
Gold Oval / Blk Rings $14
Unmarked Oval Design

NC 365
Mexico
Gold Rectangle IZZY $40
Unmarked Smooth Gold Back

NC 366
Mexico
Gold Rectangle / Trchmk $15
No Backstamp. Smooth Gold Back.

Sorry, Photo of This Pin Is Not Available

NC367

Sorry, Photo of This Pin Is Not Available

NC368

Sorry, Photo of This Pin Is Not Available

NC369

NC370

Sorry, Photo of This Pin Is Not Available

NC371

NC372

Sorry, Photo of This Pin Is Not Available

NC373

NC374

NC375

NC376

NC377

NC378

NC 367	Mexico	Green Circle	$30	
NC 368	Mexico	"IMSS"	$12	
NC 369	Mexico	Map	$12	
NC 370	Mexico	Oval Torch & Flag	$12	CABRE F MEX®. Various pictograms are also stamped on back
NC 371	Mexico	Red Circle	$30	
NC 372	Mexico	Tombstne Trchmk & Flg	$20	CABRI F MEX
NC 373	Mexico	Torch & Eagle	$12	
NC 374	Mexico	Upside Dn Tombstone	$20	Unmarked Smooth Gold Back
NC 375	Mexico	Yellow Circle	$30	
NC 376	Moldova	Crown- Envoy	$21	
NC 377	Moldova	Dated Round Crown	$15	HO HO NYC/CHINA
NC 378	Moldova	Generic Round Crown	$21	HO HO NYC/CHINA

NC379

NC380

NC381

NC382

NC383

NC384

NC385

NC386

NC387

NC388

NC389

NC390

NC 379
Moldova
White Rec / Crown Pin — $17
Unmarked Crosshatch Grid

NC 380
Monaco
Dated Shield — $8
MONACO/TM,©1992 ACOG/36 USC
380/Pin SocietyExclusive/AMINCO/CHINA

NC 381
Monaco
Gold Circle/Shield 1896-1996 — $20
No Backstamp. Semi-Smooth Gold Back.

NC 382
Monaco
Two Flags / Torchmk — $18
No Backstamp. Semi-Smooth Gold back.

NC 383
Mongolia
Cut-out Filled Rings — $35
Unmarked Crosshatch Grid

NC 384
Mongolia
Flag — $45
Unmarked Smooth Gold Back
Pin for "Atlanta" backstamped "Yoleen"

NC 385
Morocco
Burgundy Oval — $5
MOROCCO NOC/LIMITED TO 500

NC 386
Morocco
Crn / Top of Trchmrk — $50
No Backstamp. Smooth Gold back.

NC 387
Morocco
Crown on Rings — $20
No Backstamp. Smooth Gold back.

NC 388
Morocco
Sm Crown Inside Oval — $40
Unmarked Smooth Gold Back

NC 389
Morocco
Sm Crwn/Triangle Rngs — $30
Unmarked Smooth Gold Back

NC 390
Mozambique
Red Triangle — $25
G.C.I./MADE IN TAIWAN

NC391

NC392

NC393

NC394

NC395

NC396

NC397

NC398

NC399

NC400

Sorry, Photo of This Pin Is Not Available

NC401

NC402

NC 391 — Mozambique
White Triangle — $21
Unmarked Honeycomb Design

NC 392 — Myanmar
Wht. Rec./Peacock — $50
Unmarked Clear Plastic

NC 393 — Namibia
Black Circle — $8
No Backstamp. Semi-Smooth Gold Back.

NC 394 — Namibia
White Circle — $10
Unmarked Honeycomb Design

NC 395 — Nauru
White Circ - "First Oly..." — $50
No Backstamp. Smooth Gold back.

NC 396 — Nauru
White Circ / Sunburst — $33
Unmarked Smooth Gold Back

NC 397 — Nepal
Large Brnze Rec / Vill. — $50
Nepal Olympic/Committee 1998
Original

NC 398 — Nepal
Large White Rec — $50
Nepal Olympic/Committee 1998
Rejected Prototype

NC 399 — Nepal
Wht Circle / Rings — $15
NOC 1996

NC 400 — Netherlands
"NOC-NSF" Rectangle — $13
Unmarked Smooth Gold Back

NC 401 — Netherlands
White Circle / Shield — $15
Unmarked Smooth Silver Back

NC 402 — Netherlands
Windmill — $10
NETHERLANDS/TM,©1992 ACOG/36 USC 380/Pin SocietyExclusive/AMINCO/CHINA

NC403

NC404

NC405

NC406

NC407

NC408

NC409

NC410

NC411

NC412

NC413

NC414

NC 403
Netherlands Antilles
Dated "NAOC" — $28
Unmarked Smooth Gold Back

NC 404
Netherlands Antillies
White Circle / Shield — $18
Unmarked Crosshatch Grid

NC 405
New Zealand
Cutout Gold Fern Leaf/Rings — $10
No Backstamp. Smooth Gold Back.

NC 406
New Zealand
Dated Fern Leaf — $10
©NZOOCA/TM,© 1992 ACOG/36 USC 380/BY AMINCO/CHINA

NC 407
New Zealand
Dated Fern-Filled Rings — $10
Tm. ©1992 ACOG

NC 408
New Zealand
Dated Kiwi — $10
Exclusive/AMINCO/CHINA©NZOOCA/TM, © 1992 ACOG/36 USC 380/BY AMIN-CO/CHINA

NC 409
New Zealand
Generic Kiwi — $10
No Backstamp. Smooth Gold Back.

NC 410
New Zealand
Rec Fern Leaf — $12
Unmarked Crosshatch Grid

NC 411
Nicaragua
Yellow Circle — $70
Unmarked Smooth Bronzetone Back

NC 412
Niger
Purple Shield — $10
NIGER/TM,©1992 ACOG/36 USC 380/Pin SocietyExclusive/AMINCO/CHINA

NC 413
Nigeria
Green/White Shield — $14
DOMMER STUTTGART/W-GERMANY

NC 414
Nigeria
Round Shield — $18
Unmarked Smooth Gold Back

NC415

NC416

NC417

NC418

Sorry, Photo of This Pin Is Not Available

NC419

NC420

NC421

Sorry, Photo of This Pin Is Not Available

NC422

NC423

Sorry, Photo of This Pin Is Not Available

NC424

NC425

NC426

NC 415
Nigeria
Shield on Eagle — $13
NIGERIA/TM,©1992 ACOG/36 USC 380/Pin SocietyExclusive/AMINCO/CHINA

NC 416
Nigeria
Small Shield — $14
No Backstamp. Semi-Smooth Gold Back.

NC 417
North Korea
Circle / Flag — $37
Unmarked Textured Gold Back
Pin for Atlanta is smaller

NC 418
North Korea
Flag on Rectangle — $67
Unmarked Textured Gold Back

NC 419
Norway
"Olympia Toppen" Cut-Out — $20

NC 420
Norway
Rectangle / Shield — $18
Above pin: OPPLAG:10000 STK
Below pin: © 1900 N.O.K./All rights reserved

NC 421
Norway
Red Oval on Gld Bkgrnd — $14
Unmarked Crosshatch Grid

NC 422
Norway
Red Oval -Wht /Blue — $15
Unmarked Smooth Silver Back

NC 423
Norway
Shld / "Olympia ..." — $12
Above pin: Trofe/Lillehammer
Below pin: © 1900 N.O.K./All rights reserved

NC 424
Oman
Colored Circle — $
Unmarked Smooth Gold Back

NC 425
Oman
Crossed Swords — $
Unmarked Smooth Gold Back

NC 426
Oman
Dated White Circle — $
OMAN/TM,©1992 ACOG/36 USC 380/Pin SocietyExclusive/AMINCO/CHINA

NC427

NC428

NC429

NC430

NC431

NC432

NC433

NC434

Sorry, Photo of This Pin Is Not Available

NC435

NC436

NC437

Sorry, Photo of This Pin Is Not Available

NC438

NC 427 — Oman

Gold Circle | $

Unmarked Smooth Gold Back

NC 428 — Oman

Oval -Crossed Swords | $

Unmarked Smooth Gold Back

NC 429 — Pakistan

Blue/Gld Circ / Trchmk | $26

No Backstamp. Smooth Gold Back.

NC 430 — Pakistan

Maroon Rec / Trchmk | $28

Unmarked Smooth Gold Back

NC 431 — Palestine

Domed Grn/Wht Shld | $100

No Backstamp. Rough Gold Back.

NC 432 — Palestine

Green Shield | $51

36 USC 380/AMINCO/<Phone#>/CHINA

NC 433 — Palestine

Red & Black Shield | $48

36 USC 380/AMINCO/<Phone#>/CHINA

NC 434 — Panama

Folk Art Bird / Shield | $25

P.O.C. LICERSED/NCO ©/ARTISS REGI-NA/CANADA

NC 435 — Panama

Shield | $20

Unmarked Smooth Gold Back

NC 436 — Panama

Ship | $20

P.O.C. LICERSED/NCC©/ARTISS REGINA/CANADA

NC 437 — Papua New Guinea

Facing Birds | $30

© PNG NOC 1995/<Picture of Crown/KP

NC 438 — Papua New Guinea

Green "Delegation" | $50

NC439

NC440

NC441

NC442

NC443

NC444

NC445

NC446

NC447

NC448

NC449

NC450

NC 439 — Papua New Guinea
Irregular Octagon — $21
36 USC 380/AMINCO/<Phone#>/CHINA

NC 440 — Papua New Guinea
Yellow Bird — $18
Unmarked Crosshatch Grid

NC 441 — Paraguay
Generic Torch — $25
No Backstamp. Semi-Smooth Gold Back.

NC 442 — Peru
Red/White Shield — $14
Unmarked Smooth Gold Back

NC 443 — Peru
Silver Llama Stickpin — $20
Unmarked Smooth Silver Back

NC 444 — Peru
Waving Flag / Trchmk — $20
Unmarked Smooth Gold Back

NC 445 — Phillipines
Generic Flag & Rings — $14
No Backstamp. Rough Gold Back.

NC 446 — Poland
Dated Flag — $25
Unmarked Crosshatch Grid

NC 447 — Poland
Eagle on Torch — $10
MET

NC 448 — Poland
Flag/Rings "SPORTOWCV DZIECIOM" — $18
Unmarked Smooth Gold Back

NC 449 — Poland
Generic Flag — $12
Unmarked Smooth Gold Back

NC 450 — Poland
Globe / Cutout Torch — $15
Unmarked Smooth Gold Back

NC451

NC452

NC453

NC454

NC455

NC456

NC457

NC458

NC459

NC460

NC461

NC462

NC 451 — Poland
Olympic & Polish Flags — $20
Unmarked Smooth Gold Back
Sillouette of People Raising

NC 452 — Poland
Hands — $13
Unmarked Smooth Gold Back

NC 453 — Poland
Wht Circ / Flame — $18
Unmarked Smooth Gold Back

NC 454 — Portugal
Blue Circle / Ribbon — $40
Unmarked Smooth Gold Back
Generic version also made

NC 455 — Portugal
Large "A" & Shield — $15
Unmarked Smooth Gold Back

NC 456 — Portugal
Shield on Cutout Rngs/Portugal — $15
No Backstamp. Rough Gold Back.

NC 457 — Portugal
White Shld/Cutout Torchmk — $8
PORTUGAL/TM,©1992 ACOG/36 USC 380/Pin SocietyExclusive/AMINCO/CHINA

NC 458 — Puerto Rico
Dated Rectangle — $15
No Backstamp. Smooth Gold back.

NC 459 — Puerto Rico
Generic White Circle — $13
Unmarked Smooth Gold Back

NC 460 — Qatar
Slivertone Circle — $20
NEW ART/MILANO ITALY

NC 461 — Qatar
Torchmark Dangle — $13
Unmarked Smooth Gold Back

NC 462 — Romania
Waving Flag ("1996") — $15
Comite Olympique/Roumain

NC463

NC464

NC465

NC466

NC467

NC468

NC469

NC470

NC471

NC472

Sorry, Photo of This Pin Is Not Available

NC473

NC474

NC 463 — Romania
Waving Flag ("'96") — $21
Comite Olympique/Roumain

NC 464 — Russia
Black Rectangle — $12
Trofe/Lillehammer stamped above pin. © 1994 R.O.C./Officially licensed product.

NC 465 — Russia
Blue Rectangle — $12
Trofe/Lillehammer stamped above pin. © 1994 R.O.C./Officially licensed product.

NC 466 — Russia
Cutout ROCLogo&Rngs — $12
Unmarked Smooth Gold Back

NC 467 — Russia
Dated Flag — $25
Unmarked Smooth Silver Back

NC 468 — Russia
Eagle Pin on Brass Pin — $15
Unmarked Smooth Brass Colored Back

NC 469 — Russia
Eagle Pin on Color Pin — $15
Unmarked Smooth Brass Colored Back

NC 470 — Russia
Eagle Pin on Color Pin — $15
Unmarked Smooth Brass Colored Back

NC 471 — Russia
Eagle Pin on Color Pin — $15
Unmarked Smooth Brass Colored Back

NC 472 — Russia
Eagle Pin on Color Pin — $15
Unmarked Smooth Brass Colored Back

NC 473 — Russia
Gold Two Headed Eagle — $65

NC 474 — Russia
Onion Dome — $12
Trofe/Lillehammer stamped above pin. © 1994 R.O.C./Officially licensed product.

NC475

NC476

NC477

NC478

NC479

NC480

NC481

Sorry, Photo of This Pin Is Not Available

NC482

NC483

NC484

NC485

NC486

NC 475 — Russia

Onion Domes (Dated)	$14
ROC LICENSED/NCC ©/ARTISS REGINA/CANADA	

NC 476 — Russia

Participant (Blue)	$10
Trofe/Lillehammer above pin. ©1994 R.O.C./Official licensed product.	

NC 477 — Russia

Participant (Red)	$10
Trofe/Lillehammer above pin. ©1994 R.O.C./Official licensed product.	

NC 478 — Russia

Participant (White)	$23
Trofe/Lillehammer above pin. ©1994 R.O.C./Official licensed product.	

NC 479 — Russia

"Russian House"	$11
UNION MADE/U.S.A. inside oval on bottom left corner	

NC 480 — Russia

Waving Flag	$25
Trofe/Lillehammer stamped to right of pin. ROC 1996/Opening ceremony pin/All rights reserved	

NC 481 — Russia

White Rectangle	$15
Trofe/Lillehammer stamped above pin. © 1994 R.O.C./Officially licensed product.	

NC 482 — Rwanda

Gold "R" in Circle	$200

NC 483 — San Marino

Dated White/Blue Shld	$21
KOPPE/SAN MARINO	

NC 484 — San Marino

Gen White/Blue Shld	$13
No Backstamp. Smooth Gold Back.	

NC 485 — San Marino

Gold Medal	$9
SAN MARINO/TM,©1992 ACOG/36 USC 380/Pin SocietyExclusive/AMINCO/CHINA	

NC 486 — Saudi Arabia

Gold Circle	$24
ETALEX	

NC487

NC488

NC489

NC490

NC491

NC492

NC493

NC494

NC495

NC496

NC497

NC498

NC 487 — Saudi Arabia
Gold Swords — $17
Unmarked Smooth Gold Back

NC 488 — Senegal
Shield — $35
FRAISSE/PARIS

NC 489 — Seychelles
Large Shield — $40
Unmarked Smooth Gold Back

NC 490 — Seychelles
Small Shield — $10
SEYCHELLES/TM,©1992 ACOG/36 USC 380/Pin SocietyExclusive/AMINCO/CHINA

NC 491 — Sierra Leone
Crossed Flgs — $150
TM,©1992 ACOG/HOHO NYC/CHINA

NC 492 — Sierra Leone
Shield — $100
Unmarked Smooth Gold Back

NC 493 — Singapore
Dated Shield — $10
SINGAPORE/TM,©1992 ACOG/36 USC 380/Pin SocietyExclusive/AMINCO/CHINA

NC 494 — Singapore
Red Shield — $14
No Backstamp. Smooth Gold back.

NC 495 — Slovakia
Gold Square — $14
Unmarked Smooth Gold Back

NC 496 — Slovakia
Gold Trapezoid — $12
Unmarked Smooth Gold Back

NC 497 — Slovakia
Grn/White Trapezoid — $13
36 USC 380/SVK-NOC/LTD. 1500/AMIN-CO

NC 498 — Slovakia
Silver Square — $10
Unmarked Smooth Silver Back

NC499

NC500

NC501

NC502

NC503

NC504

NC505

NC506

NC507

NC508

NC509

NC510

NC 499 — Slovakia
Silver Trapezoid — $11
Unmarked Crosshatch Grid

NC 500 — Slovenia
Cutout Flags (100) — $9
No Backstamp. Smooth Gold Back.

NC 501 — Slovenia
Dated Cutout Flgs&Rngs — $15
SLOVENIA/TM,©1992 ACOG/36 USC 380/Pin SocietyExclusive/AMINCO/CHINA

NC 502 — Slovenia
Rec / Cutout Flags — $16
Unmarked Smooth Gold Back

NC 503 — Solomon Islands
Flg on Column / Rngs — $18
36 USC 380/IMPRINTED PRODUCTS/SAN DIEGO, CA/<Phone #>/MADE IN CHINA

NC 504 — Solomon Islands
Green Circle — $20
36 USC 380/AMINCO/<Phone#>/CHINA

NC 505 — Solomon Islands
Turtle — $32
36 USC 380/AMINCO/<Phone#>/CHINA

NC 506 — Somalia
Camel — $8
SOMALIA NOC/LIMITED EDITION/OF 2000

NC 507 — Somalia
Elephant — $8
SOMALIA NOC/LIMITED EDITION/OF 2000

NC 508 — Somalia
Giraffe — $8
SOMALIA NOC/LIMITED EDITION/OF 2000

NC 509 — Somalia
Gold Circ / Wht Star — $6
SOMALIA NOC ®/Made in Taiwan

NC 510 — Somalia
Gordon County (GA) Host — $6
SOMALIA NOC® /made in Taiwan

Sorry, Photo of This Pin Is Not Available

NC511

NC512

NC513

NC514

NC515

NC516

NC517

NC518

NC519

NC520

NC521

NC522

NC 511 — Somalia
Gordon County (GA) VIP — $6

NC 512 — Somalia
Grn Wreath / Wht Star — $6
SOMALIA/TM,©1992 ACOG/36 USC 380/Pin SocietyExclusive/AMINCO/CHINA

NC 513 — Somalia
Lion — $8
SOMALIA NOC/LIMITED EDITION/OF 2000

NC 514 — Somalia
Monkey — $8
SOMALIA NOC/LIMITED EDITION/OF 2000

NC 515 — Somalia
Rhinos — $8
SOMALIA NOC/LIMITED EDITION/OF 2000

NC 516 — Somalia
VIP Blue / Stone — $10
SOMALIA NOC/LIMITED EDITION/OF 200

NC 517 — Somalia
VIP Red / Stone — $10
SOMALIA NOC/LIMITED EDITION/OF 200

NC 518 — Somalia
VIP White / Stone — $10
SOMALIA NOC/LIMITED EDITION/OF 200

NC 519 — Somalia
Zebra — $8
SOMALIA NOC/LIMITED EDITION/OF 2000

NC 520 — South Africa
Black Circle — $10
Unmarked Diamond Design
Barcelona

NC 521 — South Africa
Black Rectangle — $21
LICENSED PRODUCT/SUPPLIED BY COL-LIS/LICENSING (PTY) LTD S.A.

NC 522 — South Africa
Dated Grn/White Rec — $18
No Backstamp. Smooth Gold back.

NC523

NC524

NC525

NC526

NC527

NC528

NC529

NC530

NC531

NC532

NC533

NC534

NC 523 — South Africa
Green/White Rectangle — $20
No Backstamp. Smooth Gold back.
Lillehammer

NC 524 — South Africa
House of Africa Dangle — $11
IMPRINTED PRODUCTS/<Phone #>/SAN DIEGO, CA/MADE IN CHINA

NC 525 — South Africa
Two Flags — $20
LICENSED PRODUCT

NC 526 — South Africa
Wht Rec / Color Rings — $17
LICENSED PRODUCT SUPPLIER/BY COLLIS LICENSING/(PTY) LTD S.A.

NC 527 — South Africa
Wht Rec / Gold Rings — $15
No Backstamp. Smooth Gold back.

NC 528 — South Korea
Dated Circ / Yin/Yang — $8

NC 529 — South Korea
Gen / Cutout Rings — $10
Unmarked Smooth Gold Back

NC 530 — South Korea
Oval / Torchmark — $14
No Backstamp. Smooth Gold back.

NC 531 — South Korea
S.Kor & US Flags B'tween Torchmk — $70
No Backstamp. Semi-Smooth Gold Back.

NC 532 — South Korea
Squares / Torchmark — $15
No Backstamp. Smooth Gold back.

NC 533 — Spain
Dated Shield — $15
No Backstamp. Smooth Gold Back.
Generic version also produced

NC 534 — Spain
Map of Spain — $8
SPAIN/TM,©1992 ACOG/36 USC 380/Pin SocietyExclusive/AMINCO/CHINA

NC535

NC536

NC537

NC538

NC539

NC540

NC541

NC542

NC543

Sorry, Photo of This Pin Is Not Available

NC544

NC545

NC546

NC 535 — Sri Lanka

Lion / Rings — $29

Unmarked Crosshatch Grid

NC 536 — St. Kitts & Nevis

Dated White Circle — $28

Unmarked Crosshatch Grid

NC 537 — St. Kitts & Nevis

Generic White Circle — $20

Unmarked Crosshatch Grid

NC 538 — St. Kitts & Nevis

Gold Circle / Flag — $30

Unmarked Smooth Gold Back

NC 539 — St. Lucia

Flag — $28

Unmarked Smooth Gold Back

NC 540 — St. Lucia

Shield — $10

ST.LUCIA/TM,©1992 ACOG/36 USC 380/Pin SocietyExclusive/AMINCO/CHINA

NC 541 — St. Vincent/Grenadines

Silver Oval/Torch & Rings in Center — $20

No Backstamp. Semi-Smooth Gold Back.

NC 542 — Sudan

Elongated Triangle — $25

Tm.© 1992 ACOG

NC 543 — Sudan

Generic Silver Circle — $

Tm.© 1992 ACOG

NC 544 — Sudan

Gold / Rounded Bottom — $20

NC 545 — Sudan

Triangle Inside Triangle — $8

SUDAN/TM,©1992 ACOG/36 USC 380/Pin SocietyExclusive/AMINCO/CHINA

NC 546 — Surinam

Blue Circle — $28

Unmarked Smooth Gold Back

NC547

NC548

NC549

NC550

NC551

NC552

NC553

NC554

NC555

NC556

Sorry, Photo of This Pin Is Not Available

NC557

NC558

NC 547
Surinam
Green Circle — $20
36 USC 380/HO HO NYC/TAIWAN

NC 548
Surinam
Red/White/Grn Circ/Wreath — $10
SURINAM/TM,©1992 ACOG/36 USC 380/Pin SocietyExclusive/AMINCO/CHINA

NC 549
Surinam
White Circle — $20
G.C.I./MADE IN TAIWAN

NC 550
Swaziland
Gold Cutout — $80
Unmarked Smooth Gold Back

NC 551
Sweden
Blue Circle — $14
Pins Design AG/<Phone #>

NC 552
Sweden
Rectangle-Nude Athlete — $18
36 USC 380/AMINCO/CHINA

NC 553
Switzerland
Mountain Cutout — $10
SWITZERLAND/TM,©1992 ACOG/36 USC 380/Pin SocietyExclusive/AMINCO/CHINA

NC 554
Switzerland
Pewter Oval — $81
IMPRINTEX/<Phone #>

NC 555
Switzerland
Shield — $14
Impritex/<phone #>

NC 556
Switzerland
Shield / US Flag — $16
Impritex/<phone #>

NC 557
Switzerland
"Swiss Olympic Sprit" — $100

NC 558
Syria
Doves — $11
MADE IN CANADA

NC559

NC560

NC561

NC562

NC563

NC564

NC 559

Syria	
Flag	$18
Unmarked Smooth Gold Back	
Domed version w/filled rings also exist	

NC 560

Tajikistan	
Lg Mnts/Wreath	$200
36 USC 380/AMINCO/ XXX/150 /<Phone #>/AMINCO	

NC 561

Tajikistan	
"Pierre de Coubertin"	$43
36 USC 380/AMINCO/<Phone#>/CHINA	

NC 562

Tajikistan	
Square Stylized Mntns	$27
Unmarked Smooth Gold Back	

NC 563

Tajikistan	
Stylized Mntns&Trchmk	$21
Trofe/Lillehammer (on top lefthand) corner • ©1994 TAJIKISTAN NOC/Official Licensed Product (at bottom)	

NC 564

Tanzania	
King Kong/Black	$7
TANZANIA NOC/LIMITED EDITION/OF 2500	

NC565

NC566

NC567

Sorry, Photo of This Pin Is Not Available

NC568

NC569

NC570

Sorry, Photo of This Pin Is Not Available

NC571

NC572

NC573

NC574

NC575

NC576

NC 565 — Tanzania
King Kong/Brown — $8
TANZANIA NOC/LIMITED EDITION/OF 2500

NC 566 — Tanzania
Lion — $9
TANZANIA NOC/LIMITED EDITION/OF 2500

NC 567 — Tanzania
Mt. Kilamanjaro — $8
TANZANIA NOC/LIMITED EDITION/OF 2500

NC 568 — Tanzania
Silver Rec / Flag — $5

NC 569 — Tanzania
White Shield — $10
TANZANIA/TM,©1992 ACOG/36 USC 380/Pin SocietyExclusive/AMINCO/CHINA

NC 570 — Thailand
Black Brooch /Elephnt — $36
Unmarked Smooth Gold Back

NC 571 — Thailand
Black Shld / Elephant — $33

NC 572 — Thailand
Gold Shld / Elephant — $33
Unmarked Smooth Gold Back

NC 573 — Thailand
Large Boat — $39
No Backstamp. Smooth Gold Back.

NC 574 — Thailand
Large Elephant — $25
Unmarked Smooth Gold Back

NC 575 — Thailand
Sm Boat — $33
No Backstamp. Smooth Gold Back.

NC 576 — Thailand
Sm Colored Elephnt 1 — $17
Unmarked Smooth Gold Back

NC577

NC578

NC579

NC580

NC581

NC582

NC583

NC584

Sorry, Photo of This Pin Is Not Available
NC585

NC586

NC587

NC588

NC 577 — Thailand
Sm Colored Elephnt 2 — $17
Unmarked Smooth Gold Back

NC 578 — Thailand
Sm Gold Elephant — $15
No Backstamp. Smooth Gold Back.

NC 579 — Togo
"TOGO" — $51
Unmarked Crosshatch Grid

NC 580 — Togo
"TOGO" in Rings — $90
SAN MAN

NC 581 — Tonga
Cutout Cross & Dove — $15
36 USC 380/IMPRINTED PRODUCTS/SAN DEIGO.CA/<Phone #>/MADE IN CHINA

NC 582 — Tonga
Dated Crest — $23
36 USC 380/IMPRINTED PRODUCTS/SAN DIEGO, CA/<Phone #>/MADE IN CHINA

NC 583 — Tonga
Gen Shild-Mirror Finish — $36
Unmarked Smooth Silver Back

NC 584 — Tonga
Red Crest Circle — $13
Unmarked Smooth Gold Back
Small domed version also made

NC 585 — Tonga
Shield — $18
Unmarked Smooth Gold Back

NC 586 — Tonga
Shield/Torchmark — $11
LIMITED EDITION/OF 800
Small domed version also made

NC 587 — Trinidad & Tobago
Two Birds — $23
No Backstamp. Semi-Smooth Gold Back.

NC 588 — Tunisia
Blue / Torchmark — $55
No Backstamp. Smooth Gold Back.

Sorry, Photo of This Pin Is Not Available

NC589

NC590

NC591

Sorry, Photo of This Pin Is Not Available

NC592

NC593

NC594

NC595

NC596

NC597

NC598

NC599

Sorry, Photo of This Pin Is Not Available

NC600

NC 589 — Tunisia
Cresent & Star — $35

NC 590 — Tunisia
Karate — $20
FTJ
Federation Pin

NC 591 — Tunisia
Small Shield / Rings — $25
Unmarked Textured Gold Back

NC 592 — Turkey
Gold Circle — $17
Unmarked Smooth Gold Back

NC 593 — Turkey
Gold Circle/Raised Rings — $22
TEKPAR stamped upside down
President's pin

NC 594 — Turkey
Red Rimmed White Circle/Flag — $12
TURKEY/TM,©1992 ACOG/36 USC 380/Pin SocietyExclusive/AMINCO/CHINA

NC 595 — Turkey
White Circle — $16
Unmarked Smooth Gold Back

NC 596 — Turkmenistan
White Button — $
Did not issue a pin

NC 597 — Uganda
Dated Shield — $11
UGANDA/TM,©1992 ACOG/36 USC 380/Pin SocietyExclusive/AMINCO/CHINA

NC 598 — Uganda
White Circle / Birds — $17
No Backstamp. Semi-Smooth Gold Back.

NC 599 — Ukraine
Blue Shield/Cyrillic — $8
Trofe/Lillehammer stamped above pin. © 1994 U.O.C./Officially licensed product.

NC 600 — Ukraine
Blue Shield/English — $8
Trofe/Lillehammer stamped above pin. © 1994 U.O.C./Officially licensed product.

NC601

NC602

NC603

NC604

NC605

NC606

NC607

NC608

NC609

NC610

NC611

NC612

NC 601 — Ukraine
Flag / Cut-Out Rings — $16
Unmarked Crosshatch Grid

NC 602 — Ukraine
Rings Pin on Flag Pin — $18
Unmarked Smooth Goldtone Back

NC 603 — Ukraine
Rounded Top/Red &Wht — $18
Unmarked Smooth Goldtone Back

NC 604 — Ukraine
Shield / Rings — $20
Unmarked Smooth Goldtone Back

NC 605 — Ukraine
Small Blue Shield — $13
Asl-35850/TAIWAN

NC 606 — Ukraine
Torchmark/Cyrillic — $11
Trofe/Lillehammer stamped vertically below pin. ©1994 U.O.C./Official licensed product stamped to right of pin.

NC 607 — Ukraine
Torchmark/English — $11
Trofe/Lillehammer stamped above pin. © 1994 U.O.C./Officially licensed product.

NC 608 — United Arab Emirates
Wht Shld / Gold Eagle — $37
Unmarked Smooth Goldtone Back

NC 609 — United States
"Chef de Mission" — $37
36 USC 380/HO HO NYC/CHINA

NC 610 — United States
Envoy — $23
36 USC 380/HO HO NYC/CHINA

NC 611 — United States
Games Prep — $32
36 USC 380/HO HO NYC/CHINA

NC 612 — United States
Gold Shield — $27
36 USC 380/Balfour

NC613

NC614

Sorry, Photo of This Pin Is Not Available

NC615

Sorry, Photo of This Pin Is Not Available

NC616

Sorry, Photo of This Pin Is Not Available

NC617

NC618

NC619

NC620

NC621

NC622

NC623

NC624

NC 613	United States	Olympic Team	$18	36 USC 380/HO HO NYC/CHINA
NC 614	United States	President	$40	36 USC 380/HO HO NYC/CHINA
NC 615	United States	Secretary General	$35	
NC 616	United States	Staff	$20	
NC 617	United States	Thanks USOC Licensees	$18	
NC 618	Uruguay	Flag	$20	Unmarked Crosshatch Grid
NC 619	Uruguay	Torchmark and Flag	$34	No Backstamp. Smooth Goldtone back.
NC 620	Uzbekistan	Blue Rec / Eagle	$16	UZBEKISTAN/TM,©1992 ACOG/36 USC 380/Pin Society Exclusive/AMINCO/CHINA
NC 621	Uzbekistan	Flag / Rings	$21	Unmarked Square Design
NC 622	Uzbekistan	Grn Rimmed Gld Circle	$63	Unmarked Smooth Goldtone Back
NC 623	Vanuatu	Generic Shield	$24	Unmarked Smooth Goldtone Back
NC 624	Vanuatu	Green/Red Wreath	$21	36 USC 380/AMINCO/<Phone#>/CHINA

NC625

NC626

Sorry, Photo of This Pin Is Not Available

NC627

NC628

NC629

NC630

NC631

NC632

NC633

NC634

NC635

NC636

NC 625 — Vanuatu

Mask / Ocean — $27

36 USC 380/AMINCO/<Phone#>CHINA

NC 626 — Venezuela

Black Rectangle — $23

NC 627 — Venezuela

Black Square — $20

Unmarked Smooth Goldtone Back

NC 628 — Venezuela

White Rectangle — $27

Unmarked Smooth Goldtone Back

NC 629 — Vietnam

Cut-out Flag — $21

Unmarked Smooth Goldtone Back

NC 630 — Vietnam

Dated Triangle — $9

VIETNAM/TM,©1992 ACOG/36 USC 380/Pin Society Exclusive/AMINCO/CHINA

NC 631 — Vietnam

Round / Flag — $23

Unmarked Crosshatch Grid

NC 632 — Virgin Islands (US)

30th Yr/Blue &Wht Circ — $20

Unmarked Smooth Goldtone Back

NC 633 — Virgin Islands (US)

Dated Blue & Wht Circle — $25

Unmarked Smooth Goldtone Back

NC 634 — Virgin Islands (US)

Dated Gold Circ/Pnk Bird — $18

® LAURIE ARTISS LTD/REGINA CALGARY/TAIWAN

NC 635 — Virgin Islands (US)

Gen Blue Circ / Eagle — $20

No Backstamp. Smooth Goldtone Back.

NC 636 — Western Samoa

Flying Fish — $31

36 USC 380/AMINCO/<Phone #>/CHINA

NC637

NC638

NC639

NC640

NC641

NC642

Sorry, Photo of This Pin Is Not Available

NC643

NC644

NC 637	Western Samoa	
	Lg White Rec / Shield	$50
	©W.S.A.S.F./ARECO CANDIAC/(QUE) CANADA	
NC 638	Western Samoa	
	Sea Horses	$26
	36 USC 380/AMINCO/CHINA	
NC 639	Yemen	
	Gold Circle / Flag	$80
	Unmarked Smooth Gold Back	
NC 640	Yugoslavia	
	Generic Gold Square	$32
	Unmarked Textured Gold Back	
NC 641	Yugoslavia	
	Generic Silver Square	$22
	Unmarked Textured Silver Back	
NC 642	Zaire	
	Lg Bronze Hand / Trch	$16
	©C.N.O.S.E '87/ARECO CANADA	
NC 643	Zaire	
	Sm Bronze Hand / Trch	$13
NC 644	Zaire	
	Sm Silver Hand / Trch	$13
	©C.N.O.S.E. '87/ARECO/CANADA	

NC645

NC646

NC647

NC648

NC649

NC 645 — Zambia

Lg Bronze Cutout Eagle	$

ARECO/CANADA on left NOC/300 on right ZAM on lower right Ring

NC 646 — Zambia

Silver Shld-Red Eagle	$30

Unmarked Smooth Gold Back

NC 647 — Zambia

Small Bronze Eagle Cut-Out	$13

NC 648 — Zambia

Small Silver Cut-Out Eagle	$15

ARECO/CANADA on left. COM/2,000 on right.

NC 649 — Zimbabwe

Star / Eagle	$10

ZIMBABWE/TM,©1992 ACOG/36 USC 380/Pin SocietyExclusive/AMINCO/CHINA

Notes

Bid Committees

BD001

BD002

BD003

BD004

BD005

BD006

BD007

BD008

BD009

BD010

BD011

BD012

BD 001 — Aosta (Italy) 1998

Goldtone Rectangle — $50

BERTONI • MILANO

BD 002 — Athens (Greece) 1996

Blue Irregular Circle — $75

Unmarked Smooth Goldtone Back

BD 003 — Athens (Greece) 1996

Bronze Irregular Circle — $50

Unmarked Smooth Bronzetone Back

BD 004 — Athens (Greece) 1996

Silver Irregular Circle — $31

A inside Circle + "950"

BD 005 — Athens (Greece) 2004

Blue Circle — $60

Unmarked Smooth Goldtone Back

BD 006 — Athens (Greece) 2004

Blue Circle Stickpin — $100

Unmarked Smooth Goldtone Back

BD 007 — Athens (Greece) 2004

Bronze Cutout Logo — $75

Unmarked Smooth Bronzetone Back

BD 008 — Athens (Greece) 2004

Gold/Silver Cutout Logo — $125

Unmarked Smooth Goldtone Back

BD 009 — Athens (Greece) 2004

Rectangle w/ Logo — $100

Unmarked Smooth Goldtone Back

BD 010 — Athens (Greece) 2004

Red/Blue Cutout Logo — $35

Unmarked Smooth Goldtone Back

BD 011 — Atlanta (USA) 1996

Cloisonné Rounded Circle of A's — $25

TAIWAN

BD 012 — Atlanta (USA) 1996

Cut-out Circle of A's (Gold) — $200

Unknown

BD013

BD014

BD015

BD016

BD017

BD018

BD019

BD020

BD021

BD022

BD023

BD024

BD 013 — Atlanta (USA) 1996
Cut-out Circle of A's (Silver) — $175
Unknown
Pewter version also produced

BD 014 — Atlanta (USA) 1996
Domed Cut-Out Circle of A's — $75

BD 015 — Atlanta (USA) 1996
Domed Rounded Circle of A's — $12
AOC 90

BD 016 — Atlanta (USA) 1996
Gold Cutout — $250
Unknown

BD 017 — Atlanta (USA) 1996
Gold Rectangle — $75
Unmarked Smooth Goldtone Back
Tie Tack

BD 018 — Atlanta (USA) 1996
Large Circle of A's W/ Drk Blue — $50
USOC 36/USC 380/© TAIWAN

BD 019 — Atlanta (USA) 1996
Large Circle of A's W/ Lgt. Blue — $50
MADE IN TAIWAN/MARYANNE ENT./LARRY GERSON ASSOC.

BD 020 — Atlanta (USA) 1996
"Live the Dream" (Dated) — $100
Unmarked Smooth Goldtone Back

BD 021 — Atlanta (USA) 1996
"Live the Dream" (Undated) — $150

BD 022 — Atlanta (USA) 1996
Paralympic Purple Sq — $25
Unmarked Smooth Goldtone Back

BD 023 — Atlanta (USA) 1996
Rectangle Circle of A's — $75
AOC 90

BD 024 — Atlanta (USA) 1996
Rec/Stylized Phoenix — $102
EDEN KOREA

BD025

BD026

BD027

BD028

BD029

BD030

BD031

BD032

BD033

BD034

BD035

BD036

BD 025 — Atlanta (USA) 1996
Small Circle of A's — $40
Unmarked Smooth Goldtone Back

BD 026 — Atlanta (USA) 1996
Stone Mountain Circle of A's — $N/A
©AOC 1991/SMP/GIFT CREAINS/MADE IN TAIWAN

BD 027 — Atlanta (USA) 1996
Tall Circle of A's — $106

BD 028 — Beijing (China) 2000
Gold Bar — $50
Unmarked Smooth Goldtone Back

BD 029 — Beijing (China) 2000
"Parsign" — $40
Unmarked Smooth Goldtone Back

BD 030 — Beijing (China) 2000
Red Circle — $50
Unmarked Smooth Goldtone Back

BD 031 — Beijing (China) 2000
Shield w/ CCTV Logo — $50
Goldtone Back w/ Diagonal Square Design

BD 032 — Beijing (China) 2000
Small Pagoda w/ "Beijing 2000" — $25
Unmarked Smooth Goldtone Back

BD 033 — Beijing (China) 2000
Thumbnail Pagoda — $13
Unmarked Smooth Goldtone Back

BD 034 — Beijing (China) 2000
White Circle — $35
Unmarked Smooth Goldtone Back
Paralympic

BD 035 — Belgrad (Yugoslavia) 1996
Gold Square w/ Castle — $250
Unmarked Smooth Goldtone Back

BD 036 — Berlin (Germany) 2000
3D Bear — $75
N/A

BD037

BD038

BD039

BD040

BD041

BD042

BD043

BD044

BD045

BD046

BD047

BD 037 — Berlin (Germany) 2000

Bear Face w/ Black Eye — $15

Unmarked Smooth Goldtone Back

BD 038 — Berlin (Germany) 2000

Bear Face w/ "Monte Carlo" — $41

Numbered pin

BD 039 — Berlin (Germany) 2000

Bear Face w/ Red Eye — $50

Unmarked Smooth Goldtone Back

BD 040 — Berlin (Germany) 2000

Bear in Santa Claus Suit — $250

GRABENHORST & VETTERLEIN/BERLIN <Phone#>

BD 041 — Berlin (Germany) 2000

Brandenburg Gate — $75

Unmarked Smooth Goldtone Back

BD 042 — Berlin (Germany) 2000

Rabbit w/ Bear Backpack — $60

GRABENHORST & VETTERLEIN/BERLIN <Phone#>

BD 043 — Berlin (Germany) 2000

Rectangle (Domed) — $20

G + V Berlin/<Phone#>

BD 044 — Berlin (Germany) 2000

Rectangle (Printing) — $20

G + V Berlin/<Phone#>

BD 045 — Brasilia (Brazil) 2000

Rounded Square — $45

Unmarked Smooth Goldtone Back

BD 046 — Buenos Aires (Argentina) 2004

Gold Rectangle — $35

Unmarked Smooth Goldtone Back

BD 047 — Buenos Aires (Argentina) 2004

White Rectangle — $13

Unmarked Smooth Goldtone Back

BD048

BD049

BD050

BD051

BD052

BD053

BD054

BD 048

Buenos Aires (Argentina) 2004

White Rectangle Upswept Wing	$N/A

Unmarked Smooth Goldtone Back

Issued by Dept of Tourism. Not a bid pin

BD 049

Cape Town (South Africa) 2004

"2004" Puzzle Set	$50

LICENSED PRODUCT/SUPPLIED BY/COL-LIS LICENSING (PTY) LTD S.A.

BD 050

Cape Town (South Africa) 2004

Africa Gold Bkgrnd	$15

LICENSED PRODUCT/SUPPLIED BY/COL-LIS LICENSING (PTY) LTD S.A.

Also version with "E.P." on back ($40)

BD 051

Cape Town (South Africa) 2004

Final Four Announcement	$60

LICENSED PRODUCT/SUPPLIED BY/COL-LIS LICENSING (PTY) LTD S.A.

BD 052

Cape Town (South Africa) 2004

Domed Africa Silver Background	$10

Unmarked Smooth Goldtone Back

BD 053

Cape Town (South Africa) 2004

Rough Africa Silver Background	$15

Unmarked Smooth Goldtone Back

BD 054

Graz (Austria) 2002

Diamond w/ Rings	$30

Unmarked Smooth Goldtone Back

BD055

BD056

BD057

BD058

BD059

BD060

BD061

BD062

BD063

BD064

BD065

BD066

BD 055 — Graz (Austria) 2002
Diamond w/o Rings — $35
Unmarked Smooth Goldtone Back

BD 056 — Innsbruck (Austria) 2006
Goldtone Circle — $19
Unknown

BD 057 — Istanbul (Turkey) 2000
Small White Rectangle — $21
Unmarked Smooth Goldtone Back

BD 058 — Istanbul (Turkey) 2004
Ribbon w/ "Olympist" — $14
Unmarked Smooth Goldtone Back

BD 059 — Istanbul (Turkey) 2004
Small White Rectangle — $21
Unmarked Smooth Goldtone Back

BD 060 — Jaca (Spain) 1998
White Rectangle — $31
Unmarked Smooth Goldtone Back

BD 061 — Jaca (Spain) 2002
Domed Shield (Dk Silver) — $
Unmarked Smooth Silver Back

BD 062 — Jaca (Spain) 2002
Domed Shield (Lt Silver) — $21
Unmarked Smooth Silver Back

BD 063 — Lille (France) 2004
Gold Cutout — $50
Unmarked Smooth Goldtone Back

BD 064 — Lille (France) 2004
Silver Cutout — $50
Unmarked Smooth Silver Back

BD 065 — Lille (France) 2004
Silver Rectangle — $25
Unmarked Smooth Silver Back

BD 066 — Manchester (England)
M Shaped Like Medal — $25
Unmarked Smooth Silver Back

BD067

BD068

BD069

BD070

BD071

BD072

BD073

BD074

BD075

BD076

BD077

BD078

BD 067 — Manchester (England) 2000
Blue Oval — $30
Unmarked Smooth Goldtone Back

BD 068 — Manchester (England) 2000
Paralympic Oval — $23
Unmarked Smooth Goldtone Back

BD 069 — Manchester (England) 2000
White Oval Dark Blue Flame — $20
Unmarked Smooth Goldtone Back

BD 070 — Manchester (England) 2000
White Oval Light Blue Flame — $25
Unmarked Smooth Goldtone Back

BD 071 — Melbourne (Australia) 1996
Gold Oval w/ Logo — $60
Unmarked Smooth Goldtone Back

BD 072 — Melbourne (Australia) 1996
White Oval w/ Logo — $25
Black

BD 073 — Milan (Italy) 2000
Small Circle — $35
BERTONI/MILANO

BD 074 — Milan (Italy) 2000
White Rec w/ Globe — $50
BERTONI/MILANO

BD 075 — Nagano (Japan) 1998
Diestruck White Circle & Rings — $40
NWOC

BD 076 — Nagano (Japan) 1998
Domed White Circle & Rings — $40
NWOC

BD 077 — Nagano (Japan) 1998
Gold Brooch — $300
Unmarked Smooth Goldtone Back

BD 078 — Nagano (Japan) 1998
White Circle w/o Rings — $50
Unknown

BD079

BD080

BD081

BD082

BD083

BD084

BD085

BD086

BD087

BD088

BD 079
Nagano (Japan) 1998
White Square w/ Cutout Rings $49
Japanese

BD 080
Osaka (Japan) 2008
Stylized Flower Thick Letters $25
Unmarked Smooth Goldtone Back

BD 081
Osaka (Japan) 2008
Stylized Flower Thin Letters $25
Unmarked Smooth Goldtone Back

BD 082
Ostersund (Sweden) 1998
White Circle/Yellow Rim $22
Unmarked Smooth Silver Back

BD 083
Ostersund (Sweden) 2002
White Circle $23
Unmarked Smooth Goldtone Back

BD 084
Poprad-Tatry (Slovenia) 2002
Circle w/ Mountains $15
Unmarked Smooth Silver Back

BD 085
Poprad-Tatry (Slovenia) 2002
Silver Rectangle $25
Unmarked Smooth Silver Back

BD 086
Poprad-Tatry (Slovenia) 2002
Trapezoid $25
Sunray design

BD 087
Poprad-Tatry (Slovenia) 2006
Circle w/ Mountains $15
Unmarked Smooth Silver Back

BD 088
Poprad-Tatry (Slovenia) 2006
Tombstone $20
MK
Also gold version & white mtn version ✓

BD089

BD090

BD091

BD092

BD093

BD094

BD095

BD096

BD097

BD098

BD099

BD100

BD 089 — Quebec (Canada) 2002
Calgary Bridge — $25
M inside circle/LAURIE ARTISS LTD/CALGARY-REGINA/TAIWAN

BD 090 — Quebec (Canada) 2002
Cutout Logo — $15
Unmarked Crosshatch Grid

BD 091 — Quebec (Canada) 2002
Lillehammer Bridge — $25
M inside circle/LAURIE ARTISS LTD/CALGARY-REGINA/TAIWAN

BD 092 — Quebec (Canada) 2002
Short Gold Rounded Rec — $16
PRO-PULSION/<Phone#>

BD 093 — Quebec (Canada) 2002
Silver Rectangle — $15
QUALITE QUEBEC/G.LAMOND 1995

BD 094 — Quebec (Canada) 2002
Tall Gold Rounded Rec — $22
CANDIDATURE/QUEBEC 2002

BD 095 — Rio (Brazil) 2004
Butterfly — $40
Unknown
Blue & Green Vers. also made

BD 096 — Rio (Brazil) 2004
Cutout of Brazil (Green) — $40
Unmarked Smooth Silver Back
Also in yellow, red, blue, & dk green

BD 097 — Rio (Brazil) 2004
Cutout of Brazil (Purple) — $40
Unmarked Smooth Silver Back

BD 098 — Rio (Brazil) 2004
Cutout Rings (Sm. Ver) — $45
Edit Par:/Warning System P.A./Fax <number>

BD 099 — Rio (Brazil) 2004
Cutout Rings Thick Letters — $15
36 USC 360/AMINCO/<Phone#>/CHINA

BD 100 — Rio (Brazil) 2004
Cutout Rings Thin Letteris — $15
BROCHES DO BRAZIL/<PHONE #>

BD101

BD102

BD103

BD104

BD105

BD106

BD107

BD108

BD109

BD110

BD111

BD112

BD 101 — Rio (Brazil) 2004
Cutout Rings Unauthorized | $N/A
Unknown

BD 102 — Rio (Brazil) 2004
Cutout Top | $20
Series of Vertical and Horizontal Lines

BD 103 — Rio (Brazil) 2004
Flag | $35
Unknown

BD 104 — Rio (Brazil) 2004
Oval | $35
Unknown
also in gold, grn, dk grn,red,mustard, &black

BD 105 — Rio (Brazil) 2004
Parrot/Bsktbll | $15
BROCHES DO BRASIL/<Phone#>

BD 106 — Rio (Brazil) 2004
Parrot/Judo | $15
BROCHES DO BRASIL/<Phone#>

BD 107 — Rio (Brazil) 2004
Parrot/Pole Vault | $15
BROCHES DO BRASIL/<Phone#>

BD 108 — Rio (Brazil) 2004
Parrot/Soccer | $15
BROCHES DO BRASIL/<Phone#>

BD 109 — Rio (Brazil) 2004
Parrot/Swim | $15
BROCHES DO BRASIL/<Phone#>

BD 110 — Rio (Brazil) 2004
Parrot/Torch | $15
BROCHES DO BRASIL/<Phone#>

BD 111 — Rio (Brazil) 2004
Parrot/Volleybll | $15
BROCHES DO BRASIL/<Phone#>

BD 112 — Rio (Brazil) 2004
Rectangle | $35
Unmarked Smooth Goldtone Back

BD113

BD114

BD115

BD116

BD117

BD118

BD119

BD120

BD121

BD122

BD123

BD124

BD 113
Rome (Italy) 2004
Large Colosseum $ 60

BD 114
Rome (Italy) 2004
Small Colosseum $17
Unmarked Smooth Goldtone Back
This is the "sarge print" Version

BD 115
Rome (Italy) 2004
Small Colosseum $22
Unmarked Smooth Goldtone Back
This is the "small print" version

BD 116
Salt Lake City (USA) 1998
Diamond w/ Cutout Stylized Mnts $50
USOC LICENSED S.L.O.B.C. 1989/36 USC 380/SERIES #1

BD 117
Salt Lake City (USA) 1998
White Circle $100
Unknown

BD 118
Salt Lake City (USA) 1998
"World is Welcome" $50
S.L.O.B.C. 1989/SPORT VENTURE/SERIES #1
"Americas Winter Choice.1998™"Also made

BD 119
Salt Lake City (USA) 2002
Black Rectangle $60
USOC LICENSED/S.L.O.B.C. 1992 36 USC/380 SERIES #1

BD 120
Salt Lake City (USA) 2002
Club 2002 Shield $33
Unmarked Crosshatch Grid

BD 121
Salt Lake City (USA) 2002
Cowboy Hat $200

BD 122
Salt Lake City (USA) 2002
Cutout Logo $75
Unmarked Smooth Goldtone Back

BD 123
Salt Lake City (USA) 2002
Large Black Circle $60
USOC LICENSED/S.L.O.B.C. 1992 36 USC/380 SERIES #1

BD 124
Salt Lake City (USA) 2002
"Party of the Century" $25
USOC LICENSED/SLOBC 1995/36 USC 380

BD125

BD126

BD127

BD128

BD129

BD130

BD131

BD132

BD133

BD134

BD135

BD136

BD 125 — Salt Lake City (USA) 2002

Small Black Circle — $60

Unmarked Smooth Goldtone Back

BD 126 — San Juan (Puerto Rico) 2004

Goldtone Rectangle — $17

Unmarked Smooth Goldtone Back

Also made with fuscia lettering

BD 127 — San Juan (Puerto Rico) 2004

Purple Swirl — $14

Unmarked Crosshatch Grid

BD 128 — San Juan (Puerto Rico) 2004

White Square — $15

Unmarked Smooth Goldtone Back

BD 129 — Seville (Spain) 2004

Flower w/ Rings — $18

Unmarked Smooth Silver Back

BD 130 — Seville (Spain) 2004

Flower w/o Rings — $24

Unmarked Smooth Silver Back

BD 131 — Sion (Switzerland) 2002

"CONGRATULATIONS OESTERSUND" — $40

"Quebec" & "Salt Lake City" vers. produced

BD 132 — Sion (Switzerland) 2002

I (heart) Sion/Blinkie — $60

Light blink on and off

BD 133 — Sion (Switzerland) 2002

I (heart) Sion/Rectangle — $40

BD 134 — Sion (Switzerland) 2002

"DIE POST" — $35

COLLECTION SION 2002/<Phone#>/© 1994

"La Poste" Version also made

BD 135 — Sion (Switzerland) 2002

Gold Star on Tall Base — $45

COLLECTION SION 2002/<Phone#>/© 1994

Also with colored rings

BD 136 — Sion (Switzerland) 2002

"Olympia Kandidatur" — $35

Unknown

BD137

BD138

BD139

BD140

BD141

BD142

BD143

BD144

BD145

BD146

BD147

BD148

BD 137
Sion (Switzerland) 2002
Star/Gold Back $20
COLLECTION SION 2002/<Phone#>/© 1994

BD 138
Sion (Switzerland) 2002
"WELCOME" $20
TRAMONDI WERBUNG AG SWITZERLAND/Official Licensed Product worldwide/<Phone #>/© 1994 © 1995

BD 139
Sochi (Russia) 2002
White Rectangle $18
BERTONI/MILANO

BD 140
St. Petersburg (Russia) 2004
Circle $18
© 1994 R.O.C./Official licensed product

BD 141
St. Petersburg (Russia) 2004
Rectangle $23
Unmarked Smooth Goldtone Back

BD 142
St. Petersburg (Russia) 2004
Square $25
Unknown

BD 143
Stockholm (Sweden) 2004
Blue Oval w/ Gold Pegasus $45
Unmarked Smooth Goldtone Back

BD 144
Stockholm (Sweden) 2004
Blue Oval w/ Silver Pegasus $20
Unmarked Smooth Goldtone Back

BD 145
Stockholm (Sweden) 2004
Blue Rec w/ Color Pegasus $100
PINS FACTORY AB/<Phone#>/BEKRANGAD UPPLAGA./500 EX,

BD 146
Stockholm (Sweden) 2004
Blue Rec w/ Gold Pegasus $20
PINS FACTORY AB/<Phone#>/BEKRANGAD UPPLAGA./500 EX,

BD 147
Stockholm (Sweden) 2004
Blue Rec w/ Silver Pegasus $20
PINS FACTORY AB/<Phone#>/BEKRANGAD UPPLAGA./500 EX,

BD 148
Stockholm (Sweden) 2004
Cutout Pegasus w/ Rings $17
SPORRONG

SPECTOR's... ...Pins of the World

BD149

BD150

BD151

BD152

BD153

BD154

BD155

BD156

BD157

BD158

BD159

BD160

BD 149 — Stockholm (Sweden) 2004
Cutout Pegasus w/o Rings — $28
Unmarked Smooth Goldtone Back

BD 150 — Stockholm (Sweden) 2004
Founding Assoc. — $20
PINS FACTORY/<Phone#>
Luftfartsverket

BD 151 — Stockholm (Sweden) 2004
Founding Assoc. — $25
PINS FACTORY/<Phone#>
Paterna Security

BD 152 — Stockholm (Sweden) 2004
Founding Assoc. — $20
PINS FACTORY/<Phone#>
SAS Airways

BD 153 — Stockholm (Sweden) 2004
Founding Assoc. — $25
PINS FACTORY/<Phone#>
SE Banken

BD 154 — Stockholm (Sweden) 2004
Founding Assoc. — $35
PINS FACTORY/<Phone#>
SJ

BD 155 — Stockholm (Sweden) 2004
Founding Assoc. — $25
PINS FACTORY/<Phone#>
Telia

BD 156 — Stockholm (Sweden) 2004
Founding Assoc. — $35
PINS FACTORY/<Phone#>
Trygg Hansa

BD 157 — Stockholm (Sweden) 2004
Founding Assoc. — $20
PINS FACTORY/<Phone#>
Volvo

BD 158 — Stockholm (Sweden) 2004
Goldtone Rectangle — $25
PINS FACTORY AB/<Phone#>/BEKRAN-GAD UPPLAGA./500 EX.

BD 159 — Stockholm (Sweden) 2004
Map — $15
PINS FACTORY/<Phone#>

BD 160 — Stockholm (Sweden) 2004
Selected Supplier — $50
PINS FACTORY AB/<Phone#>/BEKRAN-GAD UPPLAGA./500 EX.
Pins Factory

BD161

BD162

BD163

BD164

BD165

BD166

BD167

BD168

BD169

BD170

BD171

BD172

BD 161 — Stockholm (Sweden) 2004
White Rec w/ Blue Pegasus $14
PINS FACTORY/<Phone#>

BD 162 — Sydney (Australia) 2000
Athletes-Archery $28
© SO 2000 BL 1991 TM/PINSTOP
<Phone#>

BD 163 — Sydney (Australia) 2000
Athletes-Boxing $28
© SO 2000 BL 1991 TM/PINSTOP
<Phone#>

BD 164 — Sydney (Australia) 2000
Athletes-Cycling $28
© SO 2000 BL 1991 TM/PINSTOP
<Phone#>

BD 165 — Sydney (Australia) 2000
Athletes-Cycling Teams $28
© SO 2000 BL 1991 TM/PINSTOP
<Phone#>

BD 166 — Sydney (Australia) 2000
Athletes-Equestrian $28
© SO 2000 BL 1991 TM/PINSTOP
<Phone#>

BD 167 — Sydney (Australia) 2000
Athletes-Fencing $28
© SO 2000 BL 1991 TM/PINSTOP
<Phone#>

BD 168 — Sydney (Australia) 2000
Athletes-Field Hockey $28
© SO 2000 BL 1991 TM/PINSTOP
<Phone#>

BD 169 — Sydney (Australia) 2000
Athletes-Gymnastics $28
© SO 2000 BL 1991 TM/PINSTOP
<Phone#>

BD 170 — Sydney (Australia) 2000
Athletes-High Jump $28
© SO 2000 BL 1991 TM/PINSTOP
<Phone#>

BD 171 — Sydney (Australia) 2000
Athletes-Rowing $28
© SO 2000 BL 1991 TM/PINSTOP
<Phone#>

BD 172 — Sydney (Australia) 2000
Athletes-Shotput $28
© SO 2000 BL 1991 TM/PINSTOP
<Phone#>

BD173

BD174

BD175

BD176

BD177

BD178

BD179

BD180

BD181

BD182

BD183

BD184

BD 173 Sydney (Australia) 2000
Athletes-Tennis $28
© SO 2000 BL 1991 TM/PINSTOP
<Phone#>

BD 174 Sydney (Australia) 2000
Athletes-Track and Field $28
© SO 2000 BL 1991 TM/PINSTOP
<Phone#>

BD 175 Sydney (Australia) 2000
Athletes-Volleyball $28
© SO 2000 BL 1991 TM/PINSTOP
<Phone#>

BD 176 Sydney (Australia) 2000
Crossed Flags (Austr & Bid) $22
© SO 2000 BL/1991 TM

BD 177 Sydney (Australia) 2000
Crossed Flags (McD's & Bid) $25
Unmarked Smooth Goldtone Back

BD 178 Sydney (Australia) 2000
Crossed Flags (Telestra & Bid) $25
Unmarked Smooth Goldtone Back
"Phillips" version also made

BD 179 Sydney (Australia) 2000
Cutout Wave/Blue Base $24
© SO 2000 BL 1991 TM/PINSTOP
<Phone#>

BD 180 Sydney (Australia) 2000
Cutout Wave/Silver Base $
Unknown

BD 181 Sydney (Australia) 2000
Lg Blk Circle w/ Cutout Wave $22
BENSON HOUSE/<Phone#>/© SO 2000 BL/1991

BD 182 Sydney (Australia) 2000
Lg Blk Circ w/ Cutout Wave & Rings $28
© SO 2000 BL 1991 TM/ADVANGE BADGES/AUSTRALIA/<Phone#>

BD 183 Sydney (Australia) 2000
Lg Blk Circle /Gld Cutout Wave $28
© SO 2000 BL 1991 TM

BD 184 Sydney (Australia) 2000
Lg Gld Circ w/ Cutout Wave $28
© SO 2000 BL 1991 TM/ADVANGE BADGES/AUSTRALIA/<Phone#>

BD185

BD186

BD187

BD188

BD189

BD190

BD191

BD192

BD193

BD194

BD195

BD196

BD 185 — Sydney (Australia) 2000

Lg White Circle / Cutout Wave — $28

BENSON HOUSE/<Phone#>/© SO 2000 BL/1991

BD 186 — Sydney (Australia) 2000

Lg White Circle / Wave & Rings — $22

© SO 2000 BL 1991 TM/ADVANGE BADGES/AUSTRALIA/<Phone#>

BD 187 — Sydney (Australia) 2000

Small Black Circle — $22

© SO 2000 BL 1991 TM

BD 188 — Sydney (Australia) 2000

Small Black Circle — $N/A

©AOC/SYDNEY/OLYMPICS 2000

Counterfeit

BD 189 — Sydney (Australia) 2000

Sm Blk Circle / Color Cutout — $21

© SO 2000 BL 1991 TM

BD 190 — Sydney (Australia) 2000

Sm Black Circle / Gold Cutout — $22

© SO 2000 BL 1991 TM

BD 191 — Sydney (Australia) 2000

Sm Gold Circle/Cutout Wave — $22

© SO 2000 BL 1991 TM

BD 192 — Sydney (Australia) 2000

Small White Circle — $22

© SO 2000 BL 1991 TM

BD 193 — Sydney (Australia) 2000

Small White Circle — $N/A

©AOC/SYDNEY/OLYMPICS 2000

Counterfeit

BD 194 — Sydney (Australia) 2000

Sm White Circle/Cutout Wave — $22

© SO 2000 BL 1991 TM

BD 195 — Sydney (Australia) 2000

Waves on Blue Bkgrnd — $25

© SO 2000 BL 1991 TM/PINSTOP <Phone#>

BD 196 — Sydney (Australia) 2000

Waves on Yellow Bkgrnd — $25

© SO 2000 BL 1991 TM/PINSTOP <Phone#>

BD197

BD198

BD199

BD200

BD201

BD202

BD203

BD204

BD205

BD206

BD207

BD208

BD 197 — Sydney (Australia) 2000
Waves w/ "Sydney 2000" — $25
© SO 2000 BL 1991 TM/PINSTOP <Phone#>

BD 198 — Tarvisio (Italy) 2002
Bronzetone Rounded Rec — $22
Unmarked Smooth Bronzetone Back

BD 199 — Tarvisio (Italy) 2002
"Senza Confini — $
DESIGN CENTER/<Phone#>

BD 200 — Tarvisio (Italy) 2002
Black Cursive — $25
Unmarked Smooth Black Back

BD 201 — Tarvisio (Italy) 2002
Black Print — $20
Unmarked Smooth Black Back

BD 202 — Tarvisio (Italy) 2002
Blue Print — $22
DESIGN CENTER/<Phone#>

BD 203 — Tarvisio (Italy) 2002
Wide Rounded Rec — $31
Unmarked Smooth Black Back

BD 204 — Texas (USA) 2008
"Large" Cutout — $60
Gallery Furniture

BD 205 — Texas (USA) 2008
"Small" Cutout — $35
Unmarked Smooth Silver Back

BD 206 — Toronto (Canada) 1996
Horiz "Toronto" / "JWG" — $60
©COA 1986
Lg. Horizontal "Toronto" w/

BD 207 — Toronto (Canada) 1996
Gold Rings — $20
TM in circle + "TOOC"/"M" in circle + "COA"

BD 208 — Toronto (Canada) 1996
Sm Horiz. "Toronto" (Dk Bl) — $18
©COA 1986

BD209

BD210

BD211

BD212